the
JOY
in
PRAISING
GOD

the
JOY
in
PRAISING
GOD

charles spurgeon

Whitaker House

Scripture quotations are taken from the *King James Version* (KJV) of the Holy Bible.

THE JOY IN PRAISING GOD

ISBN: 0-88368-566-3
Printed in the United States of America
Copyright © 1995 by Whitaker House

Whitaker House
30 Hunt Valley Circle
New Kensington, PA 15068

1 2 3 4 5 6 7 8 9 10 11 12 13 / 07 06 05 04 03 02 01 00 99

Contents

Chapter 1

Awakening Praise

"Awake, awake, Deborah: awake, awake, utter a song: arise, Barak, and lead thy captivity captive, thou son of Abinoam."
—Judges 5:12

Many of the saints of God are as mournful as if they were captives in Babylon, for their lives are spent in tears and sighing. They will not chant the joyous psalm of praise. If anyone requires of them a song, they reply, "How can we sing the Lord's song in a strange land?" However, we are not captives in Babylon. We do not sit down to weep by Babel's streams. The Lord has broken our captivity. He has brought us up out of our house of bondage. We are free men, not slaves. We have not been sold into the hand of cruel taskmasters, but *"we which have believed do enter into rest"* (Hebrews 4:3).

Moses could not give rest to Israel. He could bring them to Jordan, but he could not conduct them across the stream. Joshua alone could lead them into the lot of their inheritance. Likewise, Jesus, our Joshua, has led us into the land of promise. He has brought us into a land which the Lord our God reflects, a land of hills and valleys, a land that flows with milk and honey. Though the Canaanites are still in the land and plague us sorely, yet is it all our own. God has said unto us, *"All things are yours, whether Paul, or Apollos, or Cephas, or the world, or life, or death, or things present, or things to come, all are yours, and ye are Christ's, and Christ is God's"* (1 Corinthians 3:21-23).

We are not captives, sold under sin. We are a people who *"sit every man under his vine and his fig tree, and none shall make* [us] *afraid"* (Micah 4:4). *"We* [dwell in] *a strong city; salvation will God appoint for walls and bulwarks"* (Isaiah 26:1). We have come to *"Zion, the city of our solemnities"* (Isaiah 33:20). Babylon's mourning is not suitable in Zion, which is *"beautiful for situation, the joy of the whole earth...the city of the great King"* (Psalm 48:2). *"Let us serve the Lord with gladness; come before his presence with singing"* (Psalm 100:2).

Many of God's people live as if their God were dead. Their conduct would be quite consistent if *"all the promises of God in him are* [not] *yea, and in him Amen"* (2 Corinthians 1:20) and if God were a faithless God. If Christ were not a perfect Redeemer, if the Word of

God might after all turn out to be untrue, if He had not power to keep His people, and if He had not love enough with which to hold them even to the end, then might they give way to mourning and to despair. Then might they cover their heads with ashes and wrap their loins about with sackcloth. But while God is just and true, while His promises stand as fast as the eternal mountains, while the heart of Jesus is true to His spouse, while the arm of God is unpalsied and His eye undimmed, while His covenant and His oath are unbroken and unchanged, then it is not proper or fitting for the upright to go mourning all their days. You children of God, refrain from weeping and make a joyful noise unto the Rock of your salvation. Let us come before His presence with thanksgiving, expressing our gladness in Him with psalms.

> "Your harps, ye trembling saints
> Down from the willows take;
> Loud to the praise of love divine
> Bid every string awake."

First, I will urge you to **stir up all your powers for sacred praise,** to *"awake, awake, utter a song."* In the second place, I will persuade you to **practice the sacred leading of your captivity captive**. *"Arise Barak, and lead thy captivity captive, thou son of Abinoam."*

Let us look to stirring up all our powers to praise God, according to the words of the holy woman in the text, *"Awake, awake,"* repeated yet again, *"Awake, awake."* What is there that we need to awaken if we would praise God? I reply, we ought to **arouse all the bodily powers**. Our flesh is sluggish. We have been busy with the world. Our limbs have grown fatigued. But there is power in divine joy to arouse even the body itself, to make the heavy eyelids light, to reanimate the drowsy eye, and quicken the weary brain. We should call upon our bodies to awake, especially our tongues. Let it put itself in tune like David's harp of old.

A toil-worn body often makes a mournful heart. The flesh has such a connection with the spirit that it often bows down the soul. Come, then, my flesh, I charge you, awake. Blood, leap in my veins. Heart, let your pulsings be as the joy-strokes on Miriam's timbrel! Oh, all my bodily frame, stir yourself now. Begin to magnify and bless the Lord, who made you, and who has kept you in health, and preserved you from going down into the grave.

Surely we should call on all our **mental powers** to awaken. Wake up, **memory**, and find matter for the song. Tell what God has done for me in days gone by. Fly back, thoughts, to my childhood. Sing of cradle mercies. Review my youth and its early favors. Sing of long-suffering grace, which followed my wandering and bore with my rebellions. Revive before my eyes that glad hour when first I knew the Lord. Tell again the matchless story of the never ceasing streams of mercy, which have flowed to me since then and which call for songs of loudest praise. Wake up, my **judgment**, and give measure to the music. Come forth, my **understanding**, and weigh His loving-kindness in scales and His goodness in the balances. See if you can count the small dust of His mercies. See if you can understand the unsearchable riches which He has given to you in that unspeakable gift of Christ Jesus. Count His eternal mercies to you, the treasures of that covenant which he made on your behalf, even before you were born. Sing, my understanding, sing aloud of that matchless wisdom which contrived, of that divine love which planned, and of that eternal grace which carried out the scheme of your redemption.

Awake, my **imagination**, and dance to the holy melody. Gather pictures from all worlds. Bid sun and moon stay in their courses and join in your new song. Constrain the stars to yield the music of the spheres. Put a tongue into every mountain and a voice into every wilderness. Translate the lowing of the cattle and the scream of the eagle. Hear the praise of God in the rippling of the rills, the dashing of the waterfalls, and the roaring of the sea, until all His works in all places of His dominion bless the Lord.

But especially let us cry to **all the graces of our spirits**, *"awake."* Wake up, my **love**, for you must strike the keynote and lead the strain. Awake and sing unto your beloved a song touching your Well-beloved. Give to Him choice canticles, for He in the fairest among ten thousand and altogether lovely. Come forth then with your richest music and praise the name which is an ointment poured forth. Wake up, my **hope**; join hands with your sister, love, and sing of blessings yet to come. Sing of my dying hour, when He will be with me on my couch. Sing of the rising morning when my body will leap from its tomb into its Savior's arms! Sing of the expected advent, for which you look with delight! And, O my soul, sing of that heaven which He has gone before to prepare for you, that where He is, there may His people be. (See John 14:3.)

Awake my love, awake my hope, and you my **faith**, awake also! Love has the sweetest voice; hope can thrill forth the higher notes of the sacred scale; but you, faith, with your deep resounding bass melody, you must complete the song. Sing of the promise sure and certain. Rehearse the glories of the covenant ordered in all things, and sure. Rejoice in the sure mercies of David! Sing of the goodness which will be known to your in all your trials yet to come. Sing of that blood which has sealed and ratified every word of God. Glory in that eternal faithfulness which cannot lie, and of that truth which cannot fail. You, my **patience**, utter your gentle but most joyous hymn. Sing today of how He helped you to endure in sorrow's bitterest hour. Sing of the weary way along which He has borne your feet and brought you at last to lie down in green pastures beside the still waters. Oh, all my graces, heaven-begotten as you are, praise Him who did beget you. You children of His grace, sing unto your Father's name and magnify Him who keeps you alive. Let all that is in me be stirred up to magnify and bless His holy name.

Let us **wake up the energy of all those powers**—the energy of the body, the energy of the mind, the energy of the spirit. You know what it is to do a thing coldly and weakly. We might as well not praise at all. You know also what it is to praise God passionately, to throw energy into the song and so to exalt His name. Do so, each one of you, this day. Should someone like Michal, Saul's daughter, look out of the window and see you dancing before the ark with all your might and chide you as though your praise were unseemly, say unto her, *"It was before the LORD, which chose me before thy father, and before all his house...therefore will I play before the LORD"* (2 Samuel 6:21). Tell the enemy that the God of election must be praised, that the God of redemption must be extolled, that if the very heathen leaped for joy before their gods, surely they who bow before Jehovah must adore Him with rapture and

13

with ecstasy. Go forth with joy then, with all your energies thoroughly awakened for His praise.

But you say unto me, "Why should we this day awake and sing unto our God?" There are many reasons. If your hearts are right, one will well satisfy you. Come, you children of God, and bless His dear name.

Does not all nature around you sing? If you were silent, you would be an exception to the **universal adoration**. Does not the thunder praise Him as it rolls like drums in the march of the God of armies? Does not the ocean praise Him as it claps its thousand hands? Does not the sea roar with the fullness thereof? Do not the mountains praise Him when the shaggy woods upon their summits wave in adoration? Do not the lightnings write His name in letters of fire upon the midnight darkness? Does not this world, in its unceasing revolutions, perpetually roll forth His praise? Has not the whole earth a voice, and yet will we be silent? Will man—for whom the world was made, and suns and stars were created—will he be dumb? No, let him lead the chorus. Let him be the world's high priest. While the world will be as the sacrifice, let him add his heart to it, and thus supply the fire of love which will make that sacrifice smoke towards heaven.

But, believer, will your God be praised? I ask you, will your God be praised? When men behold a hero, they fall at his feet and honor him. Garibaldi emancipated a nation, and they bowed before him and did him homage. You, Jesus, the Redeemer of the multitudes of Your elect, shall You have no song? Shall You have no triumphal entry into our hearts? Shall Your name have no glory? Shall the world love its own, but the church not honor its own Redeemer? Our God must and will be praised.

If no other heart should ever praise Him, surely mine must. If creation should forget Him, His redeemed must remember Him. Do you tell us to be silent? Oh, we cannot. Do you bid us restrain our holy mirth? Indeed you ask us to do an impossibility. He is God, and He must be extolled. He is our God, our gracious, tender, faithful God. He must have the best of our songs.

Believer, you ask, "Why should I praise Him?" Let me ask you a question, too: "Is it not **heaven's employment to praise** Him?" What can make earth more like heaven than to bring down from heaven the employment of glory and to be occupied with it here? Come, believer, when you pray, you are but a man, but when you praise, you are as an angel. When you ask favor, you are but a beggar, but when you stand up to extol, you become next of kin to cherubim and seraphim. Happy, happy day, when the glorious choristers will find their numbers swelled by the addition of a multitude from earth! Happy day when you and I will join the eternal chorus! Let us begin the music here. Let us strike some of the first notes at least. If we cannot sound the full thunders of the eternal hallelujah, let us join in as best we can. Let us make the wilderness and the solitary place rejoice, and bid the desert blossom as the rose. (See Isaiah 35:1.)

Besides, Christian, do you not know that it is a good thing for you to praise your God? Mourning weakens you. Doubts destroy your strength. Your groping among the ashes makes you of the earth, earthy. Arise, for **praise is pleasant and profitable to you**. *"The joy of the Lord is your strength"* (Nehemiah 8:10). *"Delight thyself also in the Lord and he shall give thee the desires of thine heart"* (Psalm 37:4). You grow in grace when you grow in holy joy. You are more heavenly, more spiritual, more Godlike, as you get more full of joy and peace in believing on the Lord Jesus Christ. I know some Christians are afraid of gladness, but I read, *"Let the children of Zion be joyful in their King"* (Psalm 149:2). If murmuring were a duty, some saints would never sin. If mourning were commanded by God, they would certainly be saved by works, for they are always sorrowing, and so they would keep His law. Instead, the Lord has said, *"Rejoice in the Lord alway, and again I say, Rejoice"* (Philippians 4:4). To make it still stronger, He has added, *"Rejoice evermore"* (1 Thessalonians 5:16).

But I ask you one other question, believer. You say, "Why should I awake this morning to sing to my God?" I reply to you, "Do you not have **overwhelming reasons**?" Has He not done great things for you, and are you not grateful? Has He not taken you out of the horrible pit and out of the miry clay? Has He not set your feet on the Rock and established your goings, and is there no new song in your mouth? What, are you bought with blood and yet still have a silent tongue? Were you not loved of God before the world began, but you cannot sing His praise? Are you His child, an heir of God and joint heir with Jesus Christ, and yet you have no notes of gratitude? Has He fed you this day? Did He deliver you yesterday out of many troubles? Has He been with you these thirty, forty, fifty years in the wilderness, and yet have you no mercy for which to praise Him? Shame on your ungrateful heart and your forgetful spirit. Come, pluck up courage. Think of your mercies and not of your miseries. Forget your pains awhile and think of your many deliverances. Put your feet on the neck of your doubts and fears, and stand on the Rock of your salvation. May God the Holy Ghost be your Comforter, and may you begin from this hour to utter a song of gratitude.

Someone asks, "When should I praise my God?" The answer is that all His people should praise the Lord **at all times, and give thanks at every remembrance of Him**.

Extol Him even when your souls are drowsy and your spirits are inclined to sleep. When we are awake, there is little cause to say to us four times, *"Awake, awake...awake, awake, utter a song."* But when we feel most drowsy with sorrow and our eyelids are heavy, when afflictions are pressing us down to the very dust, then is the time to sing psalms to our God and **praise Him in the very depths**. But this takes much grace, and I trust that you know that there is much grace to be had. Seek it of your divine Lord, and do not be content without it. Do not be easily cast down by troubles, nor quickly made silent because of your woes.

Think of the martyrs of old, who sang sweetly at the stake. Think of Ann Askew, of all the pains she bore for Christ, and then of her courageous praise of God in her last moments. Often she had been tortured most terribly. She lay in prison expecting death, and there she wrote a verse in old English words and rhyme:

> "I am not she that lyst
>   My anker to let fall,
> For every dryslynge myst;
>   My shippe's substancyal."

She meant in the verse that she would not stop her course and cast her anchor for every drizzling mist, because she had a ship that could bear a storm, one that could break all the waves that beat against it and joyously cut through the foam. So it will be with you. Do not give God only fair-weather songs; give Him black-tempest praises. Give Him not merely summer music, as some birds will do and then fly away; give Him winter tunes. Sing in the night like the nightingales. Praise Him in the fires. Sing His high praises even in the shadow of death, and let the tomb resound with the shouts of your sure confidence. So may you give to God what God well claims from you.

When should you praise Him? Why, praise Him when you are full of doubts, even when temptations assail you, when poverty hovers round you, and when sickness bows you down. They are cheap songs which we give to God when we are rich. It is easy enough to kiss the hand of a giving God, but to bless Him when He takes away is to bless Him indeed. To cry like Job, *"though he slay me yet will I trust in him"* (Job 13:15), or to sing like Habukkuk, *"Although the fig tree shall not blossom, neither shall fruit be in the vines; the labor of the olive shall fail, and the fields shall yield no meat; the flocks shall be cut off from the fold, and there shall be no herd in the stalls: yet will I rejoice in the Lord, I will joy in the God of my salvation"* (Habukkuk 3:17-18). Christian, you ask when you should rejoice. Today, *"Awake, awake, Deborah: awake, awake, utter a song."*

Yet once more, you reply to me, "But **how** can I praise my God?" I will be a teacher of music to you, and may the Comforter be with me. Will you think right now how great your mercies are? You are not blind, deaf, or dumb. You are not a lunatic. You are not decrepit. You are not vexed with piercing pains. You are not full of agony caused by disease. You are not going down to the grave. You are not in torment, not in hell. You are still in the land of the living, the land of love, the land of grace, the land of hope. Even if this were all, there were enough reason for you to praise your God. You are not this day what you once were, a blasphemer, a persecutor, and an injuror. The song of the drunkard is not on your lips. The lascivious desire is not in your heart. And is not this a theme for praise? Remember but a little while ago, for many of you, all these sins were your delight and joy. Must not you praise Him, you chief of sinners, whose natures have been changed, whose hearts have been renewed? Think of your iniquities, which have been put away, and your transgressions, which have been covered and not laid to your charge. Think of the privileges you enjoy: you are elect, redeemed, called, justified, sanctified, adopted, and preserved in Christ Jesus. Why, if a stone or rock could but for a moment have such privileges as these, the very hardest would melt and the dumb rock give forth "hosannas."

Will you still be silent when your mercies are so great? Let them not remain "forgotten in unthankfulness, and without praises die."

Think yet again how little are your trials after all. You have not yet resisted unto blood while striving against sin. You are poor, it is true, but then you are not sick; or you are sick, but still you are not left to wallow in sin. All afflictions are but small when once sin is put away. Compare your trials with those of many who live in your own neighborhood. Put your sufferings side by side with the sufferings of some whom you have seen on their death beds. Compare your lot with that of the martyrs who have entered into their rest. Then, you will be compelled to exclaim with Paul, *"I reckon that the sufferings of this present time are not worthy to be compared to the glory which shall be revealed in us"* (Romans 8:18).

Come, now, I implore you, by the mercies of God, to be of good cheer and rejoice in the Lord your God, if it were for no other reason than that of the brave-hearted Luther. When he had been most slandered, when the Pope had launched out a new edict against him, and when the kings of the earth had threatened him fiercely, Luther would gather together his friends and say, "Come let us sing a psalm and spite the devil." He would sing the most psalms when the world roared the most. Let us now join the great German in recalling his favorite psalm:

God is our refuge and strength, a very present help in trouble.

21

Therefore will not we fear, though the earth be removed, and though the mountains be carried into the midst of the sea;
Though the waters thereof roar and be troubled, though the mountains shake with the swelling thereof. (Psalm 46:1-3)

So, **sing to make Satan angry**. He has vexed the saints. Let us vex him.

Praise the Lord to **put the world to shame**. Never let it be said that the world can make its devotees happier than Christ can make His followers. Let your songs be so continual and so sweet, that the wicked are compelled to say, "That man's life is happier than mine. I long to exchange with him. There is a something in his religion which my life and my wicked pleasures can never afford me." Praise the Lord, saints, that sinners' mouths may be set watering after the things of God. Especially praise Him in your trials, if you would make the world wonder. Strike sinners silent and make them long to know and taste the joys of which you are a partaker.

"Alas!" says one, "I cannot sing. I have nothing to sing of, nothing external for which I could praise God." It is remarked by old commentators that the windows of Solomon's temple were narrow on the outside, but that they were broad within, and that they were so cut, that though they seemed to be only small openings, yet the light was well diffused. (See the Hebrew of 1 Kings 6:4.) So is it with the windows of a believer's joy. They may look very narrow without, but they are very wide within. There is more joy from that which is within us than from that which is outside us. God's grace within, God's love, the witness of His Spirit in our hearts, these are better themes of joy than all the corn, wine, and oil with which God sometimes increases His saints. So if you have no outward mercies, **sing of inward mercies**. If the water fails without, go to that perpetual fountain which is within your own soul. *"A good man shall be satisfied from himself"* (Proverbs 14:14). When you see no cheering providence without, yet look at grace within. *"Awake, awake, Deborah! awake, awake, utter a song."*

I do not know whether you feel as I do, but in teaching about this theme, I lament over my scantiness of words and slowness of language. If I could let my heart express itself without speech or written prose, I think with God's Spirit, I could move you indeed with joy. But I find that the language of the heart is beyond them. My mind has discovered that it cannot express the fullness of joy that is within me through the confines of human language.

I now turn to the second part of this subject, very briefly and inadequately. *"Arise, Barak, and lead thy captivity captive, thou son of Abinoam."* Understand the exact picture here. Barak had routed Sisera, Jabin's captain, and all his hosts. Deborah now exhorts Barak to celebrate his triumph. as if she were saying, "Mount your chariot, Barak, and ride through the midst of the people. Let the corpse of Sisera with Jael's nail driven through its temples be dragged behind your chariot. Let the thousand captives of the Canaanites walk with their arms bound behind them. Drive before you the ten thousand flocks of sheep and herds of cattle that you have taken as a spoil. Let their chariots of iron and all their horses be led captive in grand procession. Bring up all the treasures and the jewels of which you have stripped the slain, with their armor, shields, and spears bound up as glorious trophies. Arise, Barak, **lead captive those who led you captive, and celebrate your glorious victory**."

Beloved, this is a picture which is often used in Scripture. It is written of Christ that, *"when he ascended up on high, he led captivity captive"* (Ephesians 4:8). He led principalities and powers captive at His chariot wheels. But here is a picture for us, not concerning Christ, but concerning ourselves. We are exhorted **to lead captivity captive** today.

Come up, come up, you great hosts of sins, once my terror and dismay. Long was I your slave, you Egyptian tyrants. Long did this back smart beneath your lash when conscience was awakened. Long did these members of my body yield themselves as willing servants to obey your dictates. Come up, sins, come up, for you

24

are prisoners now. You are bound in fetters of iron—no, even more than this—you are utterly slain, consumed, destroyed. You have been covered with Jesus' blood. You have been blotted out by His mercy. You have been cast by His power into the depths of the sea. Yet would I bid your ghosts come up, slain though you be, and walk in grim procession behind my chariot. Arise, people of God, celebrate your triumph. Your sins are many, but they are all forgiven. Your iniquities are great, but they are all put away. Arise and lead captive those who led you captive—your blasphemies, your forgetfulness of God, your drunkenness, your lust, all the vast legion that once oppressed you. They are all completely destroyed. Come and look upon them, sing their death psalm, and chant the life psalm of your grateful joy. **Lead your sins captive** this very day.

Bring here, bound in chains, another host who once seemed too many for us, but whom by God's grace we have totally overcome. Arise, my trials. You have been very great and very numerous. You came against me as a great host, and you were tall and strong like the sons of Anak. O my soul, you have beaten down their strength. By the help of our God have we leaped over a wall. By His power have we broken through the troops of our troubles, our difficulties, and our fears. Come now, look back and think of all the trials you have ever encountered—death in your family, losses in your business, afflictions in your body, despair in your soul. Yet here you are, more than conquerors over them all. Come, bid them all walk now in procession. To the God of our deliverances, who has delivered us out of deep waters, who has brought us out of the burning, fiery furnace, so that the smell of fire has not passed upon us—to Him be all the glory, while we **lead our trials captive**.

Arise and let us **lead captive all our temptations**. You, dear believers, have been foully tempted to the vilest sins. Satan has shot a thousand darts at you and hurled his javelin multitudes of times. Bring out the darts and snap them before his eyes, for he has never been able to reach your heart. Come, break the bow, and cut the spear in two. Burn the chariot in the fire. *"Thy right hand, O Lord, is become glorious in power: thy right hand, O Lord, hath dashed in pieces the enemy; And in the greatness of thine excellency, thou hast overthrown them that rose up against thee"* (Exodus 15:6-7). Come, children of God, kept and preserved where so many have fallen, lead now this day your temptations captive.

I want to give you hope in the example of how the Metropolitan Tabernacle congregation has indeed led captivity captive. No single church of God existing in England for the past fifty years has had to pass through more trial than we have done. We can say, *"Thou hast caused men to ride over our heads; we went through fire and through water.'"* What has been the result of it all? *"'But thou broughtest us out into a wealthy place'* (Psalm 66:12) and set our feet in a large room. All the devices of the enemy have been of no effect."

Scarcely a day rolls over my head in which the most villainous abuse, the most fearful slander is not uttered against me both privately and by the public press. Every device is employed to put down God's minister; every lie that man can invent is hurled at me. But thus far the Lord has helped me. I have never answered any man, nor spoken a word in my own defense, from the first day until now. The effect has been this: God's people have believed nothing against me. They who fear the Lord have said as often as a new falsehood has been uttered, "This is not true concerning that man. He will not answer for himself, but God will answer for him." They have not checked our usefulness as a church. They have not thinned our congregation. That which was to be but a spasm—an enthusiasm which it was hoped would only last an hour—God has daily increased, not because of me, but because of that Gospel which I preach; not because there was anything in me, but because I came out as the exponent of straightforward, honest doctrine; and not because I speak according to the critical dictates of man, but because I seek to speak the Word simply, so that the poor may comprehend what I have to say.

27

The Lord has helped us as a church. Everything has contributed to help us. The great and terrible catastrophe, invented by Satan to overturn us, was only blessed of God to swell the stream. Now I would not shut a liar's mouth if I could, nor would I stop a slanderer if it were in my power, except so that he might not sin. All these things only aid our profit, and all these attacks do but widen the stream of usefulness. Many a sinner who has been converted to God in our church was first brought to us because of some strange anecdote, some lying tale which had been told of God's servant, the minister. I say it boasting in the Lord my God. Though I become a fool in glorying, I do lead in God's name my captivity captive. Arise! Arise! You who have followed the son of Barak, and have gone up as the thousands at his feet, arise and triumph for God is with us, and His cause will prosper. His own right arm is made bare in the eyes of all the people, and all the ends of the earth will see the salvation of our God.

As it is in this one church and in our own individual spheres, so it will be in the church at large. God's ministers are all attacked; God's truth is everywhere assailed. A terrible battle awaits us. O church of God, **remember your former victories**. Awake, ministers of Christ, and lead your captivity captive. Sing of how the idols of Greece tottered before you. Say, "Where is Diana now? Where are the gods

that made glad ancient Ephesus?" Was not
Rome's arm broken before the majesty of the
church's might? Where is Jupiter, where Saturn, where Venus? They have ceased to be.
And you Vishnu, you Brahma, you gods of
China and India, you too must fall, for this day
the sons of Jehovah arise and lead their captivity captive.

> *Come, behold the works of the Lord, what
> desolations he hath made in the earth.*
> *He maketh wars to cease unto the end of
> the earth; he breaketh the bow, he cutteth
> the spear in sunder; he burneth the chariots in the fire.*
> *Be still and know that I am God; I will be
> exalted among the heathen; I will be exalted in the earth.   (Psalm 48:8-10)*

Church of God, come forth with songs.
Come forth with shouting to your last battle.
Behold the battle of Armageddon draws near.
Blow the silver trumpets for the fight, soldiers
of the cross. Come on, come on, you besieged
hosts of hell. Strong in the strength of God
Almighty, we will dash back your ranks as the
rock breaks the waves of the sea. We will stand
against you triumphantly and tread you down
as ashes under the soles of our feet. *"Arise,
Barak, and lead thy captivity captive, thou son
of Abinoam."*

I pray to God that the joy of heart which I
feel may entice some soul to seek the same.

29

That peaceful, joyous inner state is to be found only in Christ at the foot of His dear cross. Believe on Him, sinner, and you shall be saved.

Beloved believer, may the triumphant joy to be found in the victories of winning the battle ring in your hearts today. May the Lord of Hosts grant you the ability to praise Him bountifully even in the thick of warfare when the enemy has yet to be overcome. Amen.

Chapter 2

Heavenly Adoration

"I will extol thee, my God, O King; and I will bless your name forever and ever. Every day will I bless thee; and I will praise your name forever and ever."
—Psalm 145:1-2

If I were to put to you the question, "Do you pray?" the answer would very quickly given by every Christian, "Of course I do." Suppose I then added, "And do you pray every day?" the prompt reply would be, "Yes, many times in the day. I could not live without prayer." This is no more than I would expect.

However, let me change the inquiry and ask, "Do you bless God every day? Is praise as certain and constant a practice with you as prayer?" I am not sure that the answer would be quite so certain, so generous, or so prompt. You would have to stop a little while before you gave the reply. I fear in some cases, when the reply did come, it would be, "I am afraid I have been negligent in praise." Well, dear friend, have you not been wrong? Should we omit praise any more than we omit prayer? Should not praise come daily and as many times in the day as prayer does? It strikes me that to fail in praise is as unjustifiable as to fail in prayer. I will leave it with your own heart and conscience, when you have answered the question, to see to it in the future that far more of the sweet frankincense of praise is mingled with your daily offering of prayer.

Praise is certainly not at all so common in family prayer as other forms of worship. We cannot all of us praise God in the family by joining in song, because we are not all able to carry a tune, but it would be well if we could. I agree with Matthew Henry when he says, "They that pray in the family do well; they that pray and read the Scriptures do better; but they that pray, and read, and sing do best of all." There is a completeness in that kind of family worship which is much to be desired.

Whether in the family or not, let us endeavor to be filled personally and privately with God's praise and honor all the day. Let this be our resolve: *"I will extol thee, my God, O King; and I will bless thy name forever and ever. Every day will I bless thee; and I will praise thy name forever and ever."*

Praise cannot be a second-class business for it is evidently due to God, and that in a very high degree. **A sense of justice and**

duty ought to make us praise the Lord. It is the least we can do, and in some senses it is the most that we can do, in return for the multiplied benefits which He bestows upon us. What, no harvest of praise for Him who has sent the sunshine of His love and the rain of His grace upon us? What, no revenue of praise for Him who is our gracious Lord and King? He does not exact from us any servile labor, but simply says, *"Whoso offereth praise glorifieth me"* (Psalm 50:23). Praise is good, pleasant, and delightful. Let us rank it among those debts which we would not wish to forget, but are eager to pay at once.

Praise is an act which is **preeminently characteristic of the true child of God**. The man who only pretends piety will fast twice a week, and stand in the temple and offer something like prayer. But to praise God with all the heart, this is the mark of true adoption, this is the sign and token of a heart renewed by divine grace. We lack one of the surest evidences of the pure love of God if we live without presenting praise to His blessed name.

Praising God is **singularly beneficial to ourselves**. If we had more of it, we would be greatly blessed. What would lift us so much above the trials of life, what would help us to bear the burden and heat of the day, as well as songs of praise to the Most High? The soldier marches without weariness when the band is playing spirited strains. The sailor, as he pulls the rope or lifts the anchor, utters a cheery cry to aid his toil. Let us likewise try the animating power of hymns of praise. Nothing would oil the wheels of the chariot of life so well as more praising of God. Praise would end murmuring and nurse contentment. If our mouths were filled with the praises of God, there would be no room for grumbling. Praise throws a halo of glory around the head of toil and thought. In its sunlight the basest duties of life are transfigured. Sanctified by prayer and praise, each duty is raised to a hallowed worship, akin to that of heaven. It makes us more happy, more holy, and more heavenly, when we say, *"I will extol thee, my God, O King."*

Besides, unless we praise God here, are we **preparing for our eternal employment**? All is praise in heaven. If we are strangers to that exercise, how can we hope to enter in? This life is a preparatory school, and in it we are preparing for the high calling of the perfected. Are you not eager to rehearse the everlasting hallelujahs?

"I would begin the music here,
    And so my soul should rise:
Oh, for some heavenly notes to bear
    My passions to the skies!"

Learn the essential elements of heavenly praise by the practice of joyful thanksgiving, adoring reverence, and wondering love. Then, when you step into heaven, you may take your place among the singers and say, "I have been practicing these songs for years. I have praised God while I was in a world of sin and suffering, and when I was weighed down by a feeble body. Now that I am set free from earth, sin, and the bondage of the flesh, I take up the same strain to sing more sweetly to the same Lord and God."

I wish I knew what to say that would stir up every child of God to praise. As for you that are not His children—oh, that you were such! You must be born again. You cannot really praise God till you are. *"Unto the wicked God saith, What hast you to do to declare my statutes, or that you shouldest take my covenant in thy mouth?"* (Psalm 50:16). You can offer Him no real praise while your hearts are at enmity with Him. Be reconciled to God by the death of his Son, and then you will praise Him. Let no one that has tasted that the Lord is gracious, let no one that has ever been delivered from sin by the atonement of Christ, ever fail to pay to the Lord His daily tribute of thanksgiving.

To help us in this joyful duty of praise, we will examine our text and keep to it. May the Holy Spirit instruct us by it! We have first of all **the resolve of personal loyalty**: *"I will extol thee, my God, O King...forever and ever."* David personally comes before his God and King and utters this deliberate resolution that he will praise the divine Majesty forever.

35

Note here, first, that he **pays homage to God as his King**. There is no praising God correctly if we do not see Him upon the throne, reigning with unquestioned sway. Disobedient subjects cannot praise their sovereign. You must take up the Lord's yoke—it is easy—and His burden, which is light. You must come to Him, touch His scepter, receive His mercy, and own Him as your rightful Monarch, Lawgiver, and Ruler. Where Jesus comes, He comes to reign. Where God is truly known, He is always known as supreme. Over the united kingdom of our bodies, souls, and spirits the Lord must reign with undisputed authority. What a joy it is to have such a King!

"O King," says David, and it seems to have been a sweet morsel in his mouth. He was himself a king after the earthly fashion, but to him God alone was King. Our King is no tyrant, no maker of cruel laws. He demands no crushing tribute or forced service. His *"ways are ways of pleasantness, and all* [His] *paths are peace"* (Proverbs 3:17). His laws are just and good, and *"in the keeping of them there is great reward"* (Psalm 19:11). Let others exalt that they are their own masters; our joy is that God is our King. Let others yield to this or that passion or desire; as for us, we find our freedom in complete subjection to our heavenly King. Let us praise God by loyally accepting Him as our King. Let us repeat with exaltation the hymn:

"Crown him, crown him
  King of kings, and Lord of lords."

Let us not be satisfied that He reigns over us only, but let us long for the whole earth to be filled with His glory. Let this be our daily prayer: *"Thy kingdom come. Thy will be done, in earth as it is in heaven"* (Matthew 6:10). Let us constantly ascribe to Him this praise: *"For thine is the kingdom, and the power, and the glory, forever. Amen"* (Matthew 6:13).

Also note that the psalmist, in this first sentence, praises the Lord by a **personal appropriation of God to himself by faith**: *"I will extol thee, my God."* That word *"my"* is a drop of honey. Even more, it is like Jonathan's wood, full of honey; it seems to drip from every bough. He that comes into it stands knee-deep in sweetness. *"My God"* is as high a note as an angel can reach. What is another man's God to me? He must be my God, or I will not extol Him. Dear heart, have you ever taken God to be your God? Can you say with David in another place, *"This God is our God forever and ever; he shall be our guide, even unto death"* (Psalm 48:14)?

Blessed was Thomas when he bowed down, touched his Master's wounds with his finger, and cried, *"My Lord and my God"* (John 20:28). That double-handed grip of appropriation marked the death of his painful unbelief. Can you say, "Jehovah is my God"? To us there are Father, Son, and Holy Spirit; but these are one God, and this one God is our own God. Let others worship whom they will, this God our souls adore, love, and claim to be our personal possession. O beloved, if you can say, *"My God,"* you will be bound to exalt Him! If He has given Himself to you so that you can say, *"My Beloved is mine"* (Song of Solomon 2:16), you will give yourself to Him, and you will add, *"And I am his."* Those two sentences, like two covers of a book, shut within them the full score of the music of heaven.

Observe that David is **firmly resolved to praise God**. This text has four *"I will's"* in it. Frequently it is foolish for us poor mortals to say *"I will"* because our will is so feeble and fickle. But when we resolve to praise our God, we may say, *"I will...I will...I will...I will,"* until we make a solid footing of determinations. Let me tell you that you will need to say *"I will"* a great many times, for many obstacles will hinder your resolve. There will come depression of spirit, and then you must say, *"I will extol thee, my God, O King."* Poverty, sickness, losses, and crosses may assail you, and then you must say, *"I will praise thy name forever and ever."* The devil will come to tell you that you have no interest in Christ, but you must say, *"Every day will I bless thee."* When death comes, perhaps you will be in fear of it. Then it will be incumbent upon you to cry, *"I will praise thy name forever and ever."*

"Sing, though sense and carnal reason
    Fain would stop the joyful song:
Sing, and count it highest treason
    For a saint to hold his tongue."

A bold man took this motto: "While I live, I'll crow," but our motto is, "While I live, I'll praise." An old motto was, *"Dum spiro spero,"* but the saint improves upon it and cries, *"Dum expiro spero."* Not only while I live, will I hope; but when I die, I will hope. The believer even gets beyond all that and determines, "Whether I live or die, I will praise my God. O God, my heart is fixed; I will sing and give praise."

While David is thus resolute, I want you to notice that the **resolution is strictly personal**. He says, *"I will extol thee."* Whatever others do, his own mind is made up. David was very glad when others praised God. He delighted to join with the great congregation that kept holy days, but still he was attentive to his own heart and his own praise. There is no selfishness in looking well to your own personal state and condition before the Lord. He cannot be called a selfish citizen who is very careful to render his own personal suit and service to his King. A company of persons praising God would be nothing unless each individual was sincere and earnest in the worship. The praise of the great congregation is precious in such proportion as each individual, with all his heart, is saying, *"I will extol thee, my God, O King."*

Come, my soul, I will not sit silent because so many others are singing. However many songsters there may be, they cannot sing for me. They cannot pay my **personal debt of praise**. Therefore awake, my heart, and extol your God and King. What if others refuse to sing, what if a shameful silence is observed in reference to the praises of God? Then, my heart, I must stir you even more to a double diligence, that you may with even greater zeal extol your God and King! I will sing a solo if I cannot find a choir in which I may take my part. Anyhow, my God, *"I will extol thee."* At this hour men go off to other lords and set up this and that newly made god. But as for me, my ear is bored to God's doorpost as a sign of my being His bond slave. I will not go out from His service forever. Bind the sacrifice with cords, even with cords to the horns of the altar. Whatever happens, *"I will extol thee, my God, O King."*

Now, brothers and sisters, have you been losing your own personality in the multitude? As members of a church, have you thought, "Things will continue very well without me"? Correct that mistake. Each individual must have its own note to bring to God. Let Him not have to say to you, *"Thou hast bought me no sweet cane with money; neither hast thou filled me with the fat of thy sacrifices"* (Isaiah 43:24).

40

Let us not be slow in His praise, since He has been so swift in His grace.

Once more observe that, while David is thus loyally resolving to praise God, he is **praising all the time**. The resolution to praise can only come from the man who is already praising God. When he says, *"I will extol thee,"* he is already extolling. We go from praise to praise. The heart resolves and so plants the seed. Then the life is affected, and the harvest springs up and ripens. Do not let us say, "I will extol You tomorrow," or, "I will hope to praise You when I grow old, or when I have less business on hand." No, you are this day in debt. This day admit your obligation. We cannot praise God too soon.

Our very first breath is a gift from God, and it should be spent in the Creator's praise. The early morning hour should be dedicated to praise. Do not the birds set us the example? In this matter, he gives twice who gives quickly. Let your praise follow quickly your receiving of benefits, lest even during the delay you are found guilty of ingratitude. As soon as a mercy touches our coasts, we should welcome it with acclamation. Let us copy the little chick, which lifts up its head as it drinks as if to give thanks. Our thanksgiving should echo the voice of divine loving-kindness. Before the Lord our King, let us continually rejoice as we bless Him and speak well of His name.

Thus, I have set before you the resolve of a loyal spirit. Are you loyal to your God and King? Then I charge you to glorify His name. Lift up your hearts in His praise, and in all manner of ways make His name great. Praise Him with your lips. Praise Him with your lives. Praise Him with your substance. Praise Him with every faculty and capacity. Be inventive in methods of praise: *"Sing unto the Lord a new song"* (Psalm 96:1). Bring forth the long-stored and costly alabaster box. Break it open, and pour the sweet nard upon your Redeemer's head and feet. With penitents and martyrs, extol Him! With prophets and apostles, extol Him! With saints and angels. extol Him! *"For the* LORD *is great, and greatly to be praised"* (Psalm 96:4).

Now let us examine the second clause of the text which is equally full and instructive. We have in the second part of the verse the **conclusion of an intelligent appreciation**: *"And I will bless thy name forever and ever."* Blind praise is not fit for the all-seeing God. God forbade of old the bringing of blind sacrifices to His altar. Our praise ought to have brains as well as a tongue. We ought to know who the God is whom we praise. Hence David says, *"I will bless thy name,"* by which he meant God's character, His deeds, His revealed attributes.

First, observe that David presents the **worship of inward admiration**. He knows, and therefore he blesses the divine name. What is this act of blessing? Sometimes *"bless"* would appear to be used interchangeably with *"praise."* Yet there is a difference, for it is written, *"All thy works shall praise thee, O Lord; and thy saints shall bless thee"* (Psalm 145:10). You can praise a man, and yet you may never bless him. For instance, you may praise a great artist, but he may be so ungenerous to you and others that it may never occur to you to bless him. Blessing has something in it of love and delight. It is a nearer, dearer, heartier thing than praise. Saying, *"I will bless thy name,"* is to say, "I will take an intense delight in Your name. I will lovingly rejoice in it."

The very thought of God is a source of happiness to our hearts. The more we **meditate on His character**, the more joyous we become. The Lord's name is love. He is merciful and gracious, tender and pitiful. Moreover, He is a just God, righteous, faithful, true, and holy. He is a mighty God, wise and unchanging. He is a prayer-hearing God, and He keeps His promise evermore. We would not have Him other than He is. We have a sweet contentment in God as He is revealed in Scripture. Not everybody can say this, for a great many of those who profess faith nowadays desire a god of their own making and shaping. If they find anything in Scripture concerning God that grates on their tender susceptibilities, they cannot abide it. The God that casts the wicked from His presence forever—they cannot believe in Him. They therefore make unto themselves a false deity who is indifferent to sin.

All that is revealed concerning God is to me abundantly satisfactory. If I do not comprehend its full meaning, I bow before its mystery. If I hear anything of my God which does not yield me delight, I feel that there I must be out of order with Him, either through sin or ignorance, and I say, "What I know not, teach me, Lord."

I do not doubt that perfectly holy and completely informed beings are **fully content with everything that God does** and are ready to praise Him for all. Do not our souls even now bless our Lord God, who chose us, redeemed us, and called us by His grace? Whether we view him as Maker, Provider, Savior, King, or Father, we find in Him an unfathomable sea of joy. He is God, our exceeding joy. Therefore, we sit down in holy quiet and feel our souls saying, "Bless the Lord!" He is what we would have Him to be. He is better than we could have supposed or imagined. He is the crown of delight, the climax of goodness, the sum of all perfection. As often as we see the light or feel the sun, we desire to bless the Lord's name.

I believe that when David said, *"I will bless thy name,"* he meant that he **wished well to the Lord**. To bless a person means to do that person good. By blessing us, what untold benefits the Lord bestows! We cannot bless God in such a sense as that in which He blesses us, but we would if we could. If we cannot give anything to God, we can desire that He may be known, loved, and obeyed by all men. We can wish well to His kingdom and cause in the world. We can bless Him by blessing His people, by working for the fulfillment of His purposes, by obeying His precepts, and by taking delight in His ordinances. We can bless Him by submission to His chastening hand and by gratitude for His daily benefits. Sometimes we say with the psalmist, *"O my soul, thou hast said unto the Lord, thou art my Lord: my goodness extendeth not to thee; but to the saints that are in the earth, and to the excellent, in whom is all my delight"* (Psalm 16:2-3).

If only I could wash Jesus Christ's feet! Is there any believer, man or woman, who would not aspire to that office? It is not denied you. You can wash His feet by caring for His poor people and relieving their wants. You cannot provide a feast for your Redeemer. He is not hungry, but some of His people are. Feed them! He is not thirsty, but some of His disciples are. Give them a cup of cold water in the Master's name, and He will accept it as given to Himself. Do you not feel today, you that love Him, as if you wanted to do something for Him? Arise, do it, and so bless Him. It is one of the instincts of a true Christian to wish to do something for his God and King, who has done everything for him. He loved me and gave Himself for me. Should I not give myself for Him? Oh, for perfect consecration! Oh, to bless God by laying our all upon His altar and spending our lives in His service!

It seems, dear friends, that David **studied the character and actions of God** and thus praised Him. Knowledge should lead our song. The more we know of God, the more acceptably will we bless Him through Jesus Christ. I exhort you, therefore, to acquaint yourselves with God. Study His holy Book. As in a mirror you may there see the glory of the Lord reflected, especially in the person of the Lord Jesus, who is in truth the Word, the very name of the Lord. It would be a pity that we should spoil our praises by ignorance.

They that know the name of the Lord will trust Him and will praise Him. It appears from this text that David **discovered nothing after a long study of God which would be an exception to this rule**. David does not say, "I will bless Your name in all but one thing. I have seen some point of terror in what you have revealed of Yourself, and in that thing I cannot bless You." No, without any exception he reverently adores and joyfully blesses God. All his heart is contented with all of God that is revealed. Is it so with us, beloved? I earnestly hope it is.

I beg you to notice **how intense he becomes** over this: *"I will bless thy name forever and ever."* You have heard the quaint saying of "forever and a day." Here you have a gain on it: it is "forever" and then another "forever." David says, *"I will bless thy name forever."* Is not that long enough? No, he adds, *"and ever."* Are there two forevers, two eternities? If there were fifty eternities, we would spend them all in blessing the name of the Lord our God. *"I will bless thy name forever and ever."* It would be absurd to explain this hyperbolic expression. It runs parallel with the words of Addison, when he says:

> "Through all eternity to thee
>   My song of joy I'll raise;
> But oh, eternity's too short
>   To utter all thy praise!"

Somebody found fault with that verse the other day. He said, "Eternity cannot be too short." Ah, my dear friend was not a poet, I can see. But if he could get just a spark of poetry into his soul, literalism would vanish. Truly, in poetry and in praise, the letter kills. Language is a poor vehicle of expression when the soul is on fire. Words are good things for our cool judgment, but when thoughts are full of praise, they break the back of words. How often have I felt that if I could throw my tongue away and let my heart speak without syllables and arbitrary sounds, then I might express myself! David speaks as if he **scorned to be limited by language**. He must leap even over time and possibility to find room for his heart. *"I will bless thy name forever and ever."* How I enjoy these enthusiastic expressions! It shows that when David blessed the Lord, he did it heartily. While he was musing, the fire burned. He felt like dancing before the ark. He was in much the same frame of mind as Dr. Watts when he sang:

"From thee, my God, my joys shall rise
    And run eternal rounds,
Beyond the limits of the skies
    And all created bounds."

But I must move on to the third sentence of our text, which is, the **pledge of daily remembrance**. On this I would dwell with great earnestness. If you forget my teaching, I would like you to remember this part of the text: *"Every day will I bless thee."* This does not mean that I will do it now and be done with it, or I will take a week of the year in which to praise Him and leave the other fifty-one weeks silent, but rather *"every day will I bless thee."*

All through the year I will extol my God. Why should it be so? The **greatness of the gifts which we have already received** demands it. We can never fully express our gratitude for saving grace, and therefore we must keep at it. A few years ago we were lost and dead, but we have been found and made alive again. We must praise God every day for this. We were black as night with sin, but now we are washed whiter than snow. When can we cease praising our Lord for this? He loved me and gave Himself for me. When can the day come that I will stop praising Him for this? Gethsemane and the bloody sweat, Calvary and the precious blood, when will we ever be done with praising our dear Lord for all He suffered when He bought us with His own heart's blood? No, if it were only the first mercies—the mercy of election, the mercy of redemption, the mercy of effectual calling, the mercy of adoption—we have had enough to begin with to make us sing unto the Lord every day of our lives. The light which has risen on us warms all our days with gladness. It will also light them up with praise.

Today it becomes us to sing of the mercies of yesterday. The waves of love as well as of time have washed us up on the shore of today, and the beach is strewn with love. I find myself on Sunday morning exalting because another six days' work is done, and strength has been given for it. Some of us have experienced a world of loving-kindness between one Sunday and the next. If we had never had anything else from God but what we have received during the last week, we have overwhelming reason for extolling Him today.

49

If there is any day in which we would refrain from praising God, it must not be the Lord's day, for:

"This is the day the Lord hath made,
    He calls the hours his own.
Let heaven rejoice, let earth be glad,
    And praise surround the throne."

Oh, let us magnify the Lord on the day of which it can be said:

"Today he rose and left the dead,
    And Satan's empire fell.
Today the saints his triumphs spread,
    And all his wonders tell."

When we reach Monday, will we not praise God for the blessing of Sunday? Surely you cannot have forgotten the Lord as quickly as Monday! Before you go out into the world, wash your face in the clear crystal of praise. Bury each yesterday in the fine linen and spices of thankfulness.

Each day has its own mercies and should return its praise. When Monday is over, you will have something to praise God for on Tuesday. He that watches for God's hand will never be long without seeing it. If you will only spy out God's mercies, with half an eye you will see them every day of the year. Fresh are the dews of each morning, and equally fresh are its blessings. "Fresh trouble," says one.

Praise God for the trouble, for it is a richer form of blessing. "Fresh care," says another. *"Cast all your care on him, for he careth for you"* (1 Peter 5:7), and that act will in itself bless you. "Fresh labor," says another. Yes, but fresh strength, too. There is never a night that a day does not follow it, never an affliction without its consolation. Every day you must utter the memory of His great goodness.

If we cannot praise God on any one day for what we have had that day, let us **praise Him for tomorrow**. It will be better than before. Let us learn that quaint verse:

> "And a new song is in my mouth,
>   To long-lived music set;
> Glory to thee for all the grace
>   I have not tasted yet."

Let us forestall our future and draw upon the promises. What if today I am down? Tomorrow I will be up! What if today I cast ashes on my head? Tomorrow the Lord will crown me with loving-kindness! What if today my pains trouble me? They will soon be gone! It will be all the same a hundred years from now, so let me praise God for what is within measurable distance. In a few years I will be with the angels and be with my Lord Himself. Blessed be His name! Begin to enjoy heaven now. What does Paul say? *"For our citizenship is in heaven"* (Philippians 3:20 NAS), not is going to be, but is. We belong to heaven now. Our names are enrolled among its citizens. The privileges of the new Jerusalem belong to us at this present moment. Christ is ours, and God is ours!

> "This world is ours,
>   And worlds to come;
> Earth is our lodge,
>   And heaven our home."

Therefore let us rejoice and be exceeding glad, and praise the name of God this very day. *"Every day,"* said David, *"will I bless thee."*

There is **a seasonable sense about the praising of God** every day. Praise is in season every month. When you awoke, the sunlight streamed into the windows and touched your eyelids, and you said, "Bless God. Here is a charming summer's day." Birds were singing, and flowers were pouring out their perfume. You could not help praising God. But another day it was dark at the time of your rising. You groped in the dark to find the light. A thick fog hung like a blanket over all. If you were a wise man, you said, "Come, I will not get through the day if I do not make up my mind to praise God. This is the kind of weather in which I must bless God, or else go down in despair." So you woke yourself up and began to adore the Lord. One morning you awoke after a refreshing night's rest, and you praised God for it; but on another occasion, you had tossed about through a sleepless night, and then you thanked God that the weary night was over.

You smile, dear friends, but **there is always some reason for praising God**. Certain fruits and meats are in season at special times, but the praise of God is always in season. It is good to praise the Lord in the daytime. How charming is the lark's song as it carols up to heaven's gate! It is good to bless God at night. How delicious are the liquid notes of the nightingale as it thrills the night with its music! Therefore I say to you very heartily, "Come, let us praise the Lord together, in all sorts of weather and in all sorts of places."

Sometimes I have said to myself, "During this last week I have been so full of pain that I am afraid I have forgotten to praise God as much as I should have done, and therefore I will have a double portion of it now. I will get alone and have a special time of thankful thought. I want to make up some of my debts and magnify the Lord above measure." I do not like feeling that there can ever be a day in which I have not praised Him. That day would surely be a blank in my life.

Truly the sweetest praise that ever ascends to God is that which is poured forth by saints from beds of languishing. **Praise in sad times is praise indeed**. When your dog loves you because it is dinnertime, you are not sure of him; but when somebody else tempts him with a bone and he will not leave you, though just now you struck him, then you feel that he is truly attached to you. We may learn from dogs that true affection is not dependent upon what it is just now receiving. Let us not have a cupboard love for God because of His kind providence, but let us love Him and praise Him for what He is and what He has done. Let us follow hard after Him when He seems to forsake us, and praise Him when He deals hardly with us, for this is true praise. For me, though I am not without affliction for very long, I have no fault to find with my Lord. I desire to praise Him, and praise Him, and only to praise Him. Oh, that I knew how to do it worthily! Here is my resolve: *"I will extol thee, my God, O King; and I will bless thy name forever and ever. Every day will I bless thee."*

The last sentence of the text sets forth **the hope of eternal adoration**. David here exclaims, *"And I will praise thy name forever and ever."* I am quite sure when David said that, he believed that **God is unchangeable**. If God could change, how can I be sure that He will always be worthy of my praise? David knew that what God had been, He was, and what He was, then He always would be. He had not heard the sentence, *"Jesus Christ the same yesterday, and today, and forever"* (Hebrews 13:8), nor this, *"I am the Lord, I change not; therefore ye sons of Jacob are not consumed"*

(Malachi 3:6). However, he knew the truth contained in both these verses, and therefore he said, *"I will praise thy name forever and ever."* As long as God is, He will be worthy to be praised.

Another point is also clear: David believed in **the immortality of the soul**. He says, *"I will praise thy name forever and ever."* That truth was very dimly revealed in the Old Testament, but David knew it very well. He did not expect to sleep in oblivion, but to go on praising. Therefore he said *"I will praise thy name forever and ever."* No cold hand fell upon him, and no killing voice said to him, "You shall die and never praise the Lord again." Oh, no, he looked to live forever and ever, and praise forever and ever! Such is our hope, and we will never give it up. We feel eternal life within our souls. We challenge the cold hand of death to quench the immortal flame of our love or to silence the ceaseless song of our praise. The dead cannot praise God. *"God is not the God of the dead, but of the living"* (Matthew 22:32). Among the living we are numbered through the grace of God, and we know that we will live because Jesus lives.

When death comes, it will bring no destruction to us. Though it will change the conditions of our existence, **death will not change the object of our existence**. Our tongues may be silenced for a little while, but our spirits, unaffected by the diseases of our bodies, will go on praising God in their own fashion. By and by, in the resurrection, even this poor tongue will be revived. Then body, soul, and spirit will together praise the God of resurrection and eternal glory. *"I will praise thy name forever and ever."* We will never grow weary of this hallowed exercise forever and ever. It will always be new, fresh, delightful. In heaven they never require any change beyond those blessed variations of song, those new melodies which make up the everlasting harmony. On and on, forever telling the tale which never will be fully told, the saints will praise the name of the Lord forever and ever.

Of course, dear friends, David's resolve was that he would **never cease to praise God** as long as he was here below. This is our resolve also. We may have to suspend some cherished engagements, but we will never cease from praise. At a certain period of life, a man may have to stop preaching to a large congregation. Good old John Newton declared that he would never cease preaching while he had breath in his body. I admire his holy perseverance, but it was a pity that he did not suspend his preaching, for he often wearied the people and forgot the thread of his sermon. He might have done better in another place.

Well we may cease preaching, but we must never suspend praising! The day will come when you, my dear friend, cannot go to Sunday school. I hope you will go as long as you can toddle there, but it may be that you will not be able to interest the children or that your memory will begin to fail. Even then you can go on praising the Lord. And you will, never fear. I have known old people almost forget their own names and their own children, but I have known them still to remember their Lord and Master. I have heard of one who lay dying, and his friends tried to make him remember certain things, but he shook his head. At last one said, "Do you remember the Lord Jesus?" Then the mind came into full play, the eyes brightened, and the old man eloquently praised his Savior. May our last gasp be given to the praise of the Lord.

When once we have passed through the iron gate and forded the dividing river, then we will begin to praise God in a manner more satisfactory than we can reach at present. After a nobler sort, we will sing and adore. What soaring we will attempt upon the eagle wings of love! What plunges we will take into the crystal stream of praise! I think, for a while, when we first behold the throne, we will do no more than cast our crowns at the feet of Him that loved us, and then bow down under a weight of speechless praise. We will be overwhelmed with wonder and thankfulness. When we rise to our feet again, we will join in the chorus of those redeemed by blood. We will only drop out of the song when again we feel overpowered with joyful adoration and are constrained again in holy silence to shrink to nothing before the infinite, unchanging God of love. Oh, to be there! To be there soon! We may be much nearer than we think. I cannot tell what I will do, but I know this, I want no other heaven than to praise God perfectly and eternally. Is it not so with you? A heart full of praise is heaven in the bud. Perfect praise is heaven full-blown.

Let us ask for grace from God that, if we have been deficient in praise, we may now mend our ways and put on the garments of holy adoration. This day and onward may our watchword be, "Hallelujah! Praise the Lord!"

Chapter 3

A Pattern for Praise

"When he was come nigh, even now at the descent of the mount of Olives, the whole multitude of the disciples began to rejoice and praise God with a loud voice for all the mighty works that they had seen, saying, Blessed be the King that cometh in the name of the Lord: peace in heaven, and glory in the highest. And some of the Pharisees from among the multitude said unto him, Master, rebuke thy disciples. And he answered and said unto them, I tell you that, if these should hold their peace, the stones would immediately cry out."
—Luke 19:37-40

The Savior was truly *"a man of sorrows,"* but every thoughtful person has discovered the fact that down deep in His innermost soul He must have carried an inexhaustible treasury of refined and heavenly joy. I suppose that of all the human race, there was never a man who had a deeper, purer, or more abiding peace than our Lord Jesus Christ. He was *"anointed with the oil of gladness above* [his] *fellows"* (Psalm 45:7).

Benevolence is joy. From the very nature of things, the highest benevolence must have afforded the deepest possible delight. To be engaged in the most blessed of all errands, to foresee the marvelous results of His labors in time and in eternity, and even to see around Him the fruits of the good which He had done in the healing of the sick and the raising of the dead, all must have given to such a sympathetic heart as that which beat within the bosom of the Lord Jesus Christ much secret satisfaction and joy. There were a few remarkable seasons when this joy manifested itself. *"At that hour Jesus rejoiced in spirit and said, I thank you, O Father, Lord of heaven and earth"* (Luke 10:21). Christ had His songs though it was night with Him, though His face was marred and His countenance had lost the luster of earthly happiness. Yet sometimes it was lit up with a matchless splendor of unparalleled satisfaction, as He thought upon the recompense of the reward and, in the midst of the congregation, sang His praise unto God.

In this, the Lord Jesus is a blessed picture of His church on earth. It is the day of Zion's trouble. At this hour the church expects to walk with her Lord along a thorny road. She is *"without the camp"* (Hebrews 13:13). Through much tribulation she is forcing her way to the crown. She expects to meet with reproaches. To bear the cross is her office, and to be scorned and counted an alien by her mother's children is her lot.

Yet the church has a deep well of joy, from which none can drink but her own children. There are stores of wine, oil, and corn hidden in the midst of our Jerusalem, upon which the saints of God are evermore sustained and nurtured. Sometimes, as in our Savior's case, we have our seasons of intense delight, for *"there is a river, the streams whereof shall make glad the city of our God"* (Psalm 46:4). Exiles though we are, we rejoice in our King. Yes, in Him we exceedingly rejoice, while in His name we set up our banners.

For each local assembly there is a season when we are peculiarly called upon to rejoice in God. The Lord Jesus, in the narrative before us, was going to Jerusalem. His disciples fondly hoped that He would take the throne of David and set up the long-expected kingdom. Well might they shout for joy, for the Lord was in their midst in state, riding amid the acclamations of a multitude who had been glad partakers of His goodness. Jesus Christ is in our midst today, too. The kingdom is securely His. We see the crown glittering upon His brow. He has been riding through our streets, healing our blind, raising our dead, and speaking words of comfort to our mourners. We, too, attend Him in state today. The acclamations of

61

little children are not lacking, for from the Sunday school there have come songs of converted youngsters who sing gladly, as did the children of Jerusalem long ago, *"Hosanna! Blessed is he that cometh in the name of the Lord!"* (Mark 11:9).

I want, dear friends, to stir up in all of us the spirit of holy joy, because our King is in our midst. We need to welcome Him and rejoice in Him, so that He will not lack such music as our feeble lips can produce. Therefore, I invite your attention to these four verses, by way of example, that we may take a **pattern for our praise** from this inspired description. We will observe four things: first, **delightful praise**; secondly, **appropriate song**; thirdly, **intrusive objections**; fourthly, **an unanswerable argument**.

First, observe the delightful praise found here in the thirty-seventh verse. Every word is significant in this passage and deserves the careful notice of all who would learn the lesson of how to magnify the Savior. To begin with, the praise given to Christ was **speedy praise**. The happy choristers did not wait until He entered the city, but *"when he was come nigh, even now, at the descent of the mount of Olives, the whole multitude of disciples began to rejoice."* It is well to have a quick eye to perceive occasions for gratitude. Blind unbelief and bleary-eyed thanklessness allow the favors of God to lie forgotten in unthankfulness and die without praises. They walk in the noonday of mercy and see no light to sing by. But a believing, cheerful, grateful spirit detects at once the rising of the Sun of mercy and begins to sing, even at the break of day. Christian, if you sing of the mercy you have already, you would soon have more. If twilight has made you glad, you would soon have the bliss of noon. I am certain that the church in these days has lost much by not being thankful for little blessings.

We have had many prayer meetings, but very few praise meetings. It is as if the church believes she is able to cry loud enough for her own needs to be answered, but is dumb as to music for her Lord. Her King acts to her very much as He did with the man with the one talent. That man did not lend the money for interest, and therefore it was taken away. We have not thanked Him for little mercies, and therefore even these have been removed. Churches have become barren and deserted by the Spirit of God.

Let us lift up the voice of praise to our Master because He has blessed us. We have had a continual stream of revival. The cries of sinners have sounded in our ears; every day we have seen souls converted. Benjamin's mess (see Genesis 43:34) has been set near our place at the table, we have been made to feast on royal dainties, and we have been filled with bread until we have been completely sated. Shall we not praise God? Let us not require being told twice, but let our souls begin to praise Him even now, because He has come to Jerusalem.

It strikes us at once, also, that this was **unanimous praise**. Observe not only the multitude, but *"the whole multitude of the disciples"* rejoiced and praised Him. There was not one silent tongue among the disciples, not one who withheld his song. Yet, I suppose, those disciples had their trials as we have ours. There might have been a sick wife at home, or a child withering with disease. They were doubtless poor—we know they were, indeed—and poverty is never without its pinches. They were men of like passions as ourselves. They had to struggle with inbred sin and with temptation from without. Yet there seems to have been not one who, on those grounds, excluded himself from the choir of singers on that happy day. Oh, my soul, whatever you have about you which might bow you down, be glad when you remember that Jesus Christ is glorified in the midst of His church.

Beloved, why is that harp of yours hanging on the willows? (See Psalm 137:1-2.) Have you nothing to sing about? Has He done nothing for you? If you have no personal reason for blessing God, then lend us your heart and voice to help us, for we have more praise work on hand than we can get through alone; we have more to praise Him for than we are able to discharge without extra aid. Our work of praise is too great for us, so come and help us. Sing on our behalf, if you cannot on your own. Then, perhaps, you will catch the flame and find something after all for which you, too, must bless Him.

I know there are some of you who do not feel as if you could praise God at this moment. Ask the Master to put your harp in tune. Be not silent! Do bless Him! If you cannot bless Him for temporal gifts, bless Him for the spiritual ones. If you have not of late experientially enjoyed many of these, then bless Him for what He is. For that dear face covered with the bloody sweat, for those pierced hands, for that opened side, will you not praise Him? Surely, if He had not died for me, yet I must love Him, to think of His goodness in dying for others. His kindness and the generosity of His noble heart in dying for His enemies might well provoke the most unbelieving to a song. I am, therefore, not content unless all of you will contribute your note. I would have every bird throw in its note, though some cannot imitate the lark or nightingale. Yes, I would have every tree of the forest clap its hands, and even the hyssop on the wall wave in adoration. Come, beloved, cheer up. Let dull care and dark fear be gone. Up with harps and down with doubts.

Next, it was **multitudinous**. It must be praise from *"the whole multitude."* The praise must be unanimous—not one chord out of order to spoil the tune. There is something most

inspiring and exhilarating in the noise of a
multitude singing God's praises. Sometimes,
when the congregation has been in good tune
and has sung, "Praise God from whom all
blessings flow," our music has rolled upward
like thunder to the dome and has reverberated
peal on peal. These have been the happiest
moments some of us have ever known, when
every tongue was praise and every heart was
joy. Oh, let us renew those happy times; let us
anticipate the season when the dwellers in the
East and in the West, in the North and in the
South, of every age and of every climate, will
assemble on the celestial hilltops and join the
everlasting song, extolling Jesus as Lord of all.
Jesus loves the praise of many. He loves to
hear the voices of all the bloodwashed.

> "Ten thousand thousand are their tongues,
>   But all their joys are one."

Each local church is not as many as that,
but we are counted by thousands. Therefore,
let us, *the whole multitude,* praise His name.

Still it is worthy of observation that, while
the praise was multitudinous, it was quite **se-
lect**. It was the whole multitude *of the disciples.* The Pharisees did not praise Him; they
were murmuring. All true praise must come
from true hearts. If you do not learn of Christ,
you cannot render to Him acceptable song.
These disciples, of course, were of different

sorts. Some of them had but just enlisted in the army, just learned to sit at His feet. Some had worked miracles in His name and had preached the word to others, having been called to the apostolic office. But they were all disciples. I trust that in today's church congregations, a vast majority of the people are disciples. Well, all of you—you who have lately come into His school, you who have long been in it, you who have become fathers in Israel and are teaching others, you the whole multitude of disciples—I hope, will praise God. May God grant my prayer that those of you who are not disciples might soon become so. *"Take my yoke upon you,"* He said, *"and learn of me, for I am meek and lowly in heart"* (Matthew 11:29).

A **disciple is a student**. You may not know much, but you need not know anything in coming to Christ. Christ begins with ignorance and bestows wisdom. If the only thing you know is that you know nothing, you know enough to become a disciple of Jesus. There is no matriculation necessary in order to enter into Christ's college. He takes fools and makes them know the wonders of His dying love. Oh, that you may become a disciple! "Write my name down, sir," say you to the writer with the inkhorn by his side. Henceforth, you are a humble follower of the Lamb.

Now, though I would not have those who are not disciples close their mouths whenever others sing, yet I do think there are some

67

hymns in which they would behave more honestly if they did not join, for there are some expressions which hardly ought to come from unconverted lips. Better far would it be is they would pray, *"O Lord, open thou my lips, and my mouth shall show forth thy praise"* (Psalm 51:15). You may have a very sweet voice, my friend, and may sing with admirable taste and in exquisite harmony any of the parts, but God does not accept the praise where the heart is absent. The whole multitude of the disciples whom Jesus loves are the proper persons to extol the Redeemer's name. May you, dear hearer, be among that company!

Then, in the next place, you will observe that the praise they rendered was **joyful praise**. *"The whole multitude of the disciples began to rejoice."* I hope the doctrine that Christians ought to be gloomy will soon be driven out of the universe. There are no people in the world who have such a right to be happy, nor have such cause to be joyful as the saints of the living God. All Christian duties should be done joyfully, but especially the work of praising the Lord. I have been in congregations where the tune was dolorous to the very last degree; where the rhythm was so dreadfully slow that one wondered whether they would ever be able to sing through Psalm 119, and whether, to use the expression, eternity would not be too short for them to get through it. In those places, the spirit of the people has

68

seemed to be so damp, so heavy, so dead, that we might have supposed that they had met to prepare their minds for hanging rather than for blessing the ever-gracious God.

True praise sets the heart ringing its bells and hanging out its streamers. Never hang your flag at half-mast when you praise God. No, run up every color, let every banner wave in the breeze, and let all the powers and passions of your spirit exalt and rejoice in God your Savior. We are really most horribly afraid of being too happy. Some Christians think cheerfulness a very dangerous folly, if not a ruinous vice. That joyous hymn has been altered in all the English versions:

"All people that on earth do dwell
     Sing to the Lord with cheerful voice,
Him serve with fear, his praise forth tell,
     Come ye before him and rejoice."

"Him serve with fear," says the English version, but the Scotch version has less thorniness and far more rose in it. Listen to it, and catch it's holy happiness:

"Him serve with mirth, His praise forth tell;
     Before Him exceedingly rejoice."

How do God's creatures serve Him out of doors? The birds do not sit on a Sunday with golden wings, dolefully silent on the boughs of the trees, but they sing as sweetly as may be, even though the rain drops fall. As for the newborn lambs in the field, they skip to His praise, though the season is damp and cold. Heaven and earth are lit up with gladness, so why not the hearts and houses of the saints? "Him serve with mirth." The hymnologist said it well. "Before Him exceedingly rejoice." It was joyful praise.

The next point we must see is that it was **demonstrative praise**. They praised Him with their voices and with a **loud** voice. Propriety very greatly objects to the praise which is rendered by Primitive Methodists at times. Their shouts and hallelujahs are thought by some delicate minds to be very shocking. I would not, however, join in the censure, lest I should be numbered among the Pharisees who said, *"Master, rebuke thy disciples."* I wish more people were as earnest and even as vehement as the Methodists used to be. In our Lord's day we see that the people expressed the joy which they felt. I am not sure that they expressed it in the most melodious manner, but at any rate they expressed it in a hearty, lusty shout. They altogether praised with a loud voice.

It is said of Mr. Rowland Hill that, on one occasion, someone sat on the pulpit stairs, who sang in his ears with such a sharp shrill voice that he could endure it no longer, but said to the good woman, "I wish you would be quiet." When she answered, "It comes from my heart." "Oh," said he, "pray forgive me. Sing away: sing as loudly as you will." Truly, dear friends, though one might wish there were more melody in it, yet if your music comes from the heart, we cannot object to the loudness, or we might be found objecting to that which the Savior could not and would not blame. Must we not be loud? Do you wonder that we speak out? Have not His mercies a loud tongue? Do not His kindnesses deserve to be proclaimed aloud? Were not the cries upon the cross so loud that the very rocks were rent thereby? Yet should our music be a whisper? No, as Watts declares, we should:

> "Loud as his thunders shout his praise,
> And sound it lofty as his throne."

If not with loud voices of actual sound, yet we should make the praise of God loud by our actions, which speak louder than any words. We should extol Him by such great deeds of kindness, love, self-denial, and zeal that our actions may assist our words. *"The whole multitude of the disciples began to rejoice and praise God with a loud voice."* Let me ask every Christian to do something in the praise of God to speak in some way for his Master. I would say, speak today. If you cannot with your voice, speak by act and deed, but do join in the hearty shout of all the saints of God while you praise and bless the name of our ever-gracious Lord.

The praise rendered, though very demonstrative, was very **reasonable**. The reason is given: *"for all the mighty works that they had seen."* My dear friends, we have seen many mighty works which Christ has done. I do not know what these disciples happened to have seen. It is certain that after Christ entered Jerusalem, He was lavish with His miracles. The blind were healed, the deaf had their ears opened, many of those possessed with devils were delivered, and incurable diseases gave way at His word.

We have a similar reason in a spiritual sense. *"What hath God wrought?"* (Numbers 23:23). Recently at Metropolitan Tabernacle, it has been marvelous—as the elders would tell you if they could recount what God has done—the many who have come forward during the last two weeks to tell what God has done for their souls. The Holy Spirit has met with some whom hitherto no ministry had reached. Some have been convinced of sin who were wrapped up in self-righteous rags. Others have been comforted whose despondent hearts were near despair. I am sure those men who sat with inquirers must have been astonished when they found hundreds coming to talk about the things that make for their peace. It was blessed work, I doubt not, for them. They, therefore, would lead the praise. But you have all in your measure seen something of it.

During the meetings we have held we have enjoyed an overpowering sense of the divine presence. Without excitement there has been a holy bowing of spirit, and yet a blessed lifting up of hope, joy, and holy fervor. The Master has cast sweet smiles upon His church. He has come near to His beloved; He has given her the tokens of His affection and made her rejoice with joy unspeakable. Any joy which we have towards Christ will be reasonable enough, for we have seen His mighty works.

The reason for their joy was a **personal** one. There is no praise to God so sweet as that which flows from the man who has tasted that the Lord is gracious. Some of you hare been converted during the last two or three months. You must bless Him, and you will. You must take the front row now and bless His name for the mighty work which you have seen in yourself. The things which once were dear you now abhor, and those things which seemed dry and empty are now sweet and full of savor. God has turned your darkness into light. He has brought you up out of the horrible pit, out of the miry clay, and has set your feet upon a rock. Will not your established goings yield Him a grateful song? You will bless Him.

Others have had their own children saved. God has looked on one family and then another, and has taken one, two, or three. He has been pleased to lay His hand on many parents and bless their families. Oh, sing unto His name! Sing praises for the mighty works which we have seen. This will be unimpressive talk enough to those of you who have not seen it. But those who have will feel the tears starting to their eyes as they think of son and daughter, of whom they can say, *"Behold, he prayeth"* (Acts 9:11).

Saints of God, I wish I could snatch a firebrand from the altar of praise that burns before the great throne of God with which to fire your hearts, but it is the Master's work to do it. May He do it now. May every one of you feel as if you could cast your crown at His feet, as if you could sing like the cherubim and the seraphim, as if you could not yield even the first place of gratitude to the brightest spirit before the eternal throne. Right now may it be truly said, *"The whole multitude of the disciples rejoiced with a loud voice for all the mighty things which they had seen."*

> "O come, loud anthems let us sing
>   Loud thanks to our Almighty King;
> For we our voices high should raise,
>   When our salvation's rock we praise.
>
> "Into his presence let us haste
>   To thank him for his favors past;
> To him address, in joyful songs
>   The praise that to his name belongs."

We will now go on to the second point: their praise found expression in an **appropriate song**: *"Blessed be the King that cometh in the name of the Lord. Peace in heaven, and glory in the highest."*

It was an appropriate song, if you will remember that it had **Christ for its subject**. *"My heart is indicting of a good matter: I speak of the things which I have made touching the king"* (Psalm 45:1). No song is so sweet from believing lips as that which tells of Him who loved us and who gave Himself for us. This particular song sings of Christ in His character of King—a very royal song then—a melody fit for a coronation day. Crown Him! Crown Him Lord of all! This was the refrain: *"Blessed be the King."* It sang of that King as commissioned by the Most High, *"who cometh in the name of the Lord."* To think of Christ as bearing divine authority, as coming down to men in God our Father's name, speaking what He has heard in heaven, fulfilling no self-willed errand, but a mission upon which the divine Father sent Him according to His purpose and decree—all this is matter for music. Bless the Lord, saints, as you remember that your Savior is the Lord's anointed: He has set Him on His throne. Jehovah, who was pleased to bruise Him, has said, *"Yet have I set my king upon my holy hill of Zion"* (Psalm 2:6). See the Godhead of your Savior. He whom you adore, the son of Mary, is the Son of God. He who rode upon a colt, the foal of an ass, did also ride on a cherub and on the wings of the wind. They spread their garments in the way and broke down branches. It was a humble triumph, but long before this, the angels had strewn His path with adoring songs. Before Him went the lightnings, coals of fire were in His track, and up from His throne went forth hailstones and coals of fire. Blessed be the King! Praise Him this day. Praise the King, divine and commissioned by His Father.

The focus of their song was, however, of **Christ present in their midst**. I do not think they would have rejoiced so loudly and sweetly if He had not been there. That was the source and center of their mirth: the King riding upon a colt, the King triumphant. They could not but be glad when He revealed Himself. Beloved, our King is here. Many times has the hymn been sung, "Arise, O King of grace, arise, and enter to thy rest!" Remember the verse:

> "O thou that art the Mighty One
> Thy sword gird on thy thigh."

And King Jesus has done so in state. He has ridden prosperously, and out of the ivory palaces His heart has been made glad. The Kings daughter, all-glorious within, standing at His right hand, cannot but be glad, too. Loud to His praise wake every string of your heart, and let your souls make the Lord Jesus the focus of your song.

This was an appropriate song, in the next place, because it had **God for its object.** They extolled God, God in Christ, when they thus lifted up their voices. They said, *"Peace in heaven, and glory in the highest."* When we extol Christ, we desire to bless the infinite majesty that gave Christ to us. *"Thanks be unto God for his unspeakable gift"* (2 Corinthians 9:16). O eternal God, we your creatures in this little world do unfeignedly bless You for that great purpose and decree by which You did choose us to be illustrious exhibits of Your majesty and love. We bless You that You did give us grace in Christ Your Son before the starry sky was spread abroad. We praise You, O God, and magnify Your name as we inquire, *"What is man, that thou art mindful of him, or the son of man, that thou visitest him?"* (Psalm 8:4). How could You lower Yourself to stoop from all the glory of Your infinity, to be made man, to suffer, to bleed, to die for us?

"Give unto the Lord, O ye mighty, give unto the Lord glory and strength. Give unto the Lord the glory that is due unto his name" (Psalm 29:1-2). Oh, that I could give place to some inspired bard, some poet of old who, standing before Him, mouth streaming with holy eloquence, would extol Him who lives but once was slain, and bless the God who sent Him here below that He might redeem unto

Himself a people who would show forth His praise.

I think this song to have been very appropriate for another reason, namely, because it had **the universe for its scope**. It was not praise inside walls as generally ours are: the multitude sang in the open air with no walls but the horizon, with no roof but the unpillared arch of heaven. Their song, though it was from heaven, did not stay there, but enclosed the world within its range. It was, *"Peace in heaven, glory in the highest."* It is very singularly like that song of the angels, that Christmas carol of the spirits from on high when Christ was born. But it differs, for the angels' song was, *"On earth, peace"* (Luke 2:14), and this at the gates of Jerusalem was, *"Peace in heaven."*

It is the nature of song to expand and spread itself. From heaven the sacred joy began when angels sang, and then the fire blazed down to earth in the words, *"On earth, peace."* But in this case the song began on earth, and so it blazed up to heaven with the words, *"Peace in heaven; glory in the highest."* Is not it a wonderful thing that a company of poor beings, such as we who are here below, can really affect the highest heavens? Every throb of gratitude which moves our hearts glows through heaven.

God can receive no actual increase of glory from His creatures, for He has infinite glory and majesty. Yet the creature manifests that glory. A grateful man here below, when his heart is all on fire with sacred love, warms heaven itself. The multitude sang of peace in heaven, as though the angels were established in their peaceful seats by the Savior, as though the war which God had waged with sin was over because the conquering King was come. Let us seek music which will be fitted for other spheres! I would begin the music here, and so my soul should rise. Oh, for some heavenly notes to bear my passions to the skies!

This praise was appropriate to the occasion, because the universe was its sphere. It seems also to have been most appropriate because it had **gratitude for its spirit**. They cried aloud, *"Blessed!" "Blessed be the King."* We cannot bless God, and yet we do bless Him, in the sense in which He blesses us. Our goodness cannot extend to Him, but we reflect the blessedness which streams from Him as light from the sun. Blessed be Jesus! Have you ever wished to make Him happier? Have you wished that you could really extol Him? Let Him be exalted! Let Him sit on high! I have almost wished selfishly that He were not so glorious as He is, so that we might help to lift Him higher. If the crushing of my body, soul, and spirit would make Him one atom more glorious, I would not only consent to the sacrifice, but bless His name that He counted me worthy to do so. All that we can do brings nothing to Him. Yet, I desire that He had His own glory.

Praise Him that He rode over our great land in triumph! If only King Jesus were as well known here now as He was once in puritanical times! If only Scotland were as loyal to Him now as in covenanting periods! Would that Jesus had His majesty visible in the eyes of all men! We pray and for this. Among the chief joys, the most joyous is to know that God has highly exalted Him and given Him a name which is above every name, that at the name of Jesus every knee should bow.

We have thus said something about the appropriateness of the song. May each of you discover such hymns as will serve to set forth your own case and show forth the mercy of God in saving you. Do not be slack in praising Him in such notes as may be most suitable to your own condition.

Thirdly—and very briefly because I am not going to give much time to these men—we have **intrusive objections**. *"Master, rebuke thy disciples."* We know that voice, the old grunt of the Pharisee. What could he do otherwise? Such is the man, and such must his communications be. While he can dare to boast, *"God, I thank thee that I am not as other men are"* (Luke 18:11), he is not likely to join in praises such as other men lift up to heaven.

But why did these Pharisees object? I suppose it was first of all because they thought there would be no praise for them. If the multitude had been saying, "Oh, these blessed Pharisees! These excellent Pharisees! What broad phylacteries! What admirable hems to their garments! How diligently and scrupulously they tithe their mint and their anise and their cumin! What a wonder that God should permit us poor vile creatures to look upon these super-excellent incarnations of virtue," there would not have been a man among them who would have said, *"Master, rebuke thy disciples."* A proud heart never praises God, for it hoards up praise for itself.

Also, the Pharisees were jealous of the people. They did not feel so happy themselves, and they could not bear that other people should be glad. They were like the elder brother who said, *"Yet you never gavest me a kid, that I might make merry with my friends"* (Luke 15:29). Was that a reason why nobody else should be merry? A very poor reason truly! Oh, if we cannot rejoice ourselves, let us stand out of the way of other people. If we have no music in our own hearts, let us not wish to stop those who have.

But I think the main point was that they were jealous of Jesus. They did not like to have Christ crowned with majesty. Certainly this is the drift of the human heart. It does not wish to see Jesus Christ extolled. If you preach morality, dry doctrine, or ceremonies, many will be glad to hear your words. However, if you preach Jesus Christ, some will say, *"Master, rebuke thy disciples!"* It was not bad advice of an old preacher to a young beginner, when he said, "Preach nothing down but sin, and preach nothing up but Christ." Let us praise nothing up but Christ. Have nothing to say about your church, say nothing about your denomination, hold your tongue about the minister, but praise Christ. The Pharisees will not like it, but that is an excellent reason to give them more of it. That which Satan does not admire, he ought to have more of. The preaching of Christ is the whip that flogs the devil; the preaching of Christ is the thunderbolt, the sound of which makes all hell shake. Let us never be silent then. We will put to confusion all our foes, if we do but extol Christ Jesus as Lord.

"Master, rebuke thy disciples!" There is not much occurring in the Christian church in the present day to elicit this kind of request from critics for Jesus Christ to rebuke. There used to be; there used to be a little of what the world calls fanaticism. A consecrated cobbler once set forth to preach the Gospel in Hindustani regions. There were men who would go preaching the Gospel among the heathen, counting not their lives dear to them. The day was when the church was so foolish as to fling away precious lives for Christ's glory. She is more prudent now. Alas for your prudence! She is so calm and quiet—no Methodist's zeal

now. Even that denomination which did seem alive has become most proper and cold, and we are so bent too.

We let the most abominable doctrines be preached, and then put our fingers to our lips and say, "There are so many good people who think so." Nothing is to be rebuked nowadays. My soul is sick of this! Oh, for the old fire again! The church will never prosper until it becomes once more on fire. Oh, for the old fanaticism, for that indeed was the Spirit of God transforming men's spirits in earnest! Oh, for the old doing and daring that risked everything and cared for nothing, except to glorify Him who shed His blood upon the cross! May we live to see such bright and holy days again! The world may murmur, but Christ will not rebuke.

We come now to the last point, namely, **an unanswerable argument**. Jesus said, *"If these should hold their peace, the very stones would immediately cry out."* I think that is very much our case. If we were not to praise God, the very stones might cry out against us. We must praise the Lord. Woe unto us if we do not! It is impossible for us to hold our tongues. Saved from hell, and be silent? Secure of heaven, and be ungrateful? Bought with precious blood, and hold our tongues! Filled with the Spirit, and not speak? From fear of feeble man, restrain the Spirit's course within our souls? God forbid. In the name of the Most

High, let such a thought be given to the winds. We watch our children being saved, the offspring of our loins brought to Christ! We see them springing up like willows by the water's edge, and yet have no awakening of song, no gladness, no delight! Oh, then we would be worse than brutes, and our hearts would have been steeled. We must praise God!

What, the King in our midst, King Jesus smiling into our souls, feasting us at His table, making His word precious to us, and we do not praise Him? If Satan could know the delight of Christ's company, He might begin to love. But we were worse than devils if we did not praise the name of Jesus! What! The King's arm made bare, His enemies subdued, His triumphant chariot rolling through our streets, and yet no song? Oh Zion, if we forget to sing, if we count not the King's triumph above our chief joy, let our right hand forget her cunning. The King is coming, His advent is drawing near, the signs of blessing are in the sky and air around, and yet no song? Oh, we must bless Him! *"Hosanna! Blessed is he that cometh in the name of the Lord!"*

But could the stones ever cry out? Yes, that they could, and if they were to speak they would have much to talk of even as we have this day. If the stones were to speak, they could tell of their **Maker**. Will we not tell of Him who made us anew, and out of stones raised up children unto Abraham? They could

84

speak of ages long since gone. The old rocks could tell of chaos and order and the handiwork of God in various stages of creation's drama. Cannot we talk of God's decrees, of God's great work in ancient times, and all that He did for His church? If the stones were to speak, they could tell of their **breaker**, how he took them from the mine and made them fit for the temple. Cannot we tell of our Creator and Maker, who broke our hearts with the hammer of His word so that He might build us into His temple? If the stones were to speak, they would tell of their **builder**, who polished them and fashioned them after the similitude of a palace. Will not we talk of our Architect and Builder, who has put us in our place in the temple of the living God? Oh, if the stones could speak, they might have a long story to tell by way of memorial, for many times has a great stone been rolled as a memorial to God. We can tell of stones of help, stones of remembrance. The broken stones of the law cry out against us, but Christ Himself, who has rolled away the stone from the door of the sepulcher, speaks for us.

The stones might well be able to cry out, but we will not let them. We will hush their noise with ours. We will break forth into sacred song and bless the majesty of the Most High all our days. Let this day and all of our days be especially consecrated to holy joys. May the Lord in infinite mercy fill your souls with rejoicing, both in practical deeds of kindness and benevolence and works of praise! Blessed be His name who lives forever and ever!

Chapter 4

A New Song for New Hearts

"And in that day thou shalt say, O Lord, I will praise thee: though thou wast angry with me, thine anger is turned away, and thou comfortedst me."
—Isaiah 12:1

This prophesy is said by some to relate to the invasion by Sennacherib. That calamity threatened to be a very terrible display of divine anger. It seemed inevitable that the Assyrian power would make an utter desolation of Judea. But God promised that He would interpose for the deliverance of His people and punish the stout heart of the king of Assyria. Then His people would say, "We will praise You: though You were angry with us, and thus sent the Assyrian monarch to chastise us, Your anger is turned away, and You comforted us."

If this is the meaning of it, it is an instance of sanctified affliction. It is a lesson to us that whenever we smart under the rod, we may look forward to the time when the rod will be withdrawn. It is also an admonition to us that when we escape from trial, we should take care to celebrate the event with grateful praise. Let us set up the pillar of memorial, let us pour the oil of gratitude upon it, and let us garland it with song, blessing the Lord whose anger endures but for a moment, but whose mercy is from everlasting to everlasting.

Others think that this text mainly relates to the latter days. It would be impossible to read Isaiah 11 without feeling that such a reference is clear. There is to be a time when the wolf will dwell with the lamb, the lion will eat straw like the ox, and the weaned child will put his hand on the viper's den. The Lord will set His hand the second time to recover the remnant of His people and repeat his wondrous works in Egypt and at the Red Sea. Then the song of Moses will be rehearsed again: *"The Lord is my strength and song, and he is become my salvation: he is my God, and I will prepare him an habitation: my father's God, and I will exalt him"* (Exodus 15:2). In that day the Jewish people, on whose head the blood of Christ has come, who these many centuries have been scattered and sifted as in a sieve throughout all nations, will be restored to their own land, the dispersed of Judah gathered from the four corners of the earth. They will participate in the glories of the millennial reign. With joy will they draw water out of the wells of salvation. In those days, when all Israel will be saved and Judah will dwell safely, the jubilant thanksgiving will be heard, *"O Lord, I will praise you, for though thou wast angry with me, thine anger is turned away, and thou comfortedst me."* All people will sing with such unanimity and undivided heart that they will sound as though they were one man and will use the singular where their numbers might require the plural. *"I will praise thee"* will be the exclamation of the once divided but then united people.

Although both of these interpretations are true, and both instructive, the text is many-sided and bears another reading. We will find out the very soul of the passage if we consider it as an illustration of what occurs to everyone of God's people when he is brought out of darkness into God's marvelous light, when he is delivered from the spirit of bondage beneath divine wrath and led by the spirit of adoption into the liberty in which Christ makes him free. In that day I am sure that these words are fulfilled. The believer then says very joyously, *"O Lord, I will praise thee: though thou wast angry with me, thine anger is turned away, and thou comfortedst me."*

Regarding the text from this point of view, we will first observe the **prelude** of this delightful song, and then we will listen to the **song itself**. First, consider the prelude of this charming song. Here are certain preliminaries to the music. They are contained in the first line of the text. *"In that day thou shalt say..."* We have the tuning of the harps, the notes of the music following after in the succeeding sentences. Much of instruction is couched in these six words of prelude.

Note that there is **a time** for that joyous song which is here recorded, *"In that day."* The term, *"that day,"* is sometimes used for a day of terror, and often for a period of blessing. The common factor to both is this, they were both days of the manifestation of divine power. *"That day,"* a day of terrible confusion for God's enemies. *"That day,"* a day of great comfort for God's friends. The day in either case is the time of the making God's arm bare and the manifestation of His strength.

Now, the day in which a man rejoices in Christ is the day in which God's power is revealed on his behalf in his heart and conscience, and the Holy Spirit subdues him to the reign of Christ. It is not always that God works with such effectual power as this in the human heart. He has His set times. Oftentimes the work of human ministry proves ineffectual: the preacher exhorts, the hearer listens, but the exhortation is not obeyed. It sometimes happens that even desires may be excited, yet nothing is accomplished: these aroused feelings prove to be as those spring blossoms on the trees which do not pollinate and fall fruitless to the ground. There is, however, an appointed time for the calling of God's elect, a set time in which the Lord visits His chosen with a power of grace which they cannot effectually resist. He makes them willing in the day of His power. It is a day in which not only is the Gospel heard, but the report is believed, because the arm of the Lord is revealed.

For everything, according to Solomon, there is a season: a time to break down and a time to build up; a time of war and a time of peace; a time to kill and a time to heal. (See Ecclesiastes 3:1-3.) Just so, there is a time for conviction and a time for consolation. With some who are in great distress of spirit, it may be God's time to wound and to kill. Their self-confidence is too vigorous, their carnal righteousness yet too lively. Their confidence must be wounded, and their righteousness must be killed; otherwise, they will not yield to grace. God does not clothe us until He has stripped us; He does not heal till He has wounded. How could He make alive those who are not dead?

There is a work of grace in the heart of digging out the old foundations before grace begins to build up our hopes. Woe to that man who builds without having the foundation dug out, for his house will fall. Woe to that man who leaps into a sudden peace without ever having felt his need of pardon, without repentance, without brokenness of spirit. He will see his hasty fruit wither before his eyes. The time when God effectually blesses is sometimes

91

called "a time of love." It is a time of deep distress to us, but it is a time of love with God, a time wisely determined in the decree and counsel of the Most High, so that healing mercy arrives at the best time to each one who is interested in the covenant.

Someone may inquire, "When do you think will be the time when God enables me to say, *'Thine anger is turned away'*?" Beloved, you can easily discern it. I believe God's time to give us comfort is usually when we are brought low, so as to confess the justice of the wrath which He is pouring on us. Humbleness of heart is one sure indication of coming peace.

A German nobleman years ago inspected the galley ships at Toulon. He saw many men condemned by the French government to perpetual toil at the galley oars for their crimes. Being a prince in much repute, he obtained the favor that he could give liberty to one of the captives. He went among them and talked to them, but found they all thought themselves wrongly treated, oppressed, and unjustly punished. At last he met with one who confessed, "In my case my sentence is a most just and even a merciful one. If I had not been imprisoned in this way, most likely I would have been executed for some still greater crime. I have been a great offender, and the law is doing nothing more than it ought in keeping me in confinement for the rest of my life." The nobleman returned to the manager and said,

"This is the only man in all this gang that I would wish to set free. I elect him for liberty."

So it is with our great Liberator, the Lord Jesus Christ, when He meets with a soul that confesses its demerit, admits the justice of divine wrath, and has not a word to say for itself, then He says, *"Thy sins, which are many, are forgiven"* (Luke 7:47-48). The time when His anger is turned away is the time when you confess the justice of His anger, and bow down and humbly entreat for mercy. Above all, the hour of grace has struck when you look alone to Christ. While you are looking to any good thing in yourself, and hoping to grow better or to do better, you are making no advances towards comfort. But when you give up in despair any hope that is grounded in yourself, and instead look away to those dear wounds of His, to that suffering humanity, the Son of God, who stooped from heaven for you, then has the day dawned in which you will say, *"O Lord, I will praise thee."* I pray earnestly that this set time to favor you may now come—the time when the rain is over and gone, and the voice of the turtle is heard in your land.

Looking at the preliminaries of this song again, notice that a word indicates the **singer**. *"In that day thou shalt say."* *"Thou"* is a singular pronoun and points out one individual. One by one we receive eternal life and peace. "You, the individual, singled out to feel in your conscience God's wrath, you are equally selected to enjoy Jehovah's love." Beloved, it is never a day of grace to us until we are taken aside from the multitude and set by ourselves. Our individuality must come out in conversion, if it never appears at any other time. So many of you fancy that it is all right with you because you live in a Christian nation. I tell you it is woe unto you, if having outward privileges, they involve you in responsibilities, but bring you no saving grace. Perhaps you believe that your family religion may help you. The erroneous practices of certain Christian churches may foster this delusion, but it is not so. There is no birthright godliness: *"Ye must be born again"* (John 3:7). The first birth will not help you, because *"That which is born of the flesh is flesh; and that which is born of the Spirit is spirit"* (John 3:6). I know you imagine that if you mingle in godly congregations, sing as they sing, and pray as they pray, it will go well with you, but it is not so. The gate of eternal life admits but one at a time. Is it not written, *"Ye shall be gathered one by one, O ye children of Israel"* (Isaiah 27:12)? Know that when the fountain is opened in the house of David for sin and for uncleanness at Christ's coming, it is declared by the prophet Zechariah:

The land shall mourn, every family apart; the family of the house of David apart, and their wives apart; the family of the house of Nathan apart, and their wives apart;

94

*The family of the house of Levi apart, and
their wives apart; the family of Shimei
apart, and their wives apart;
All the families that remain every family
apart, and their wives apart.*
                    (Zechariah 12:12-14)

Each one of you must be brought to feel
the divine anger in your souls and to have it
removed from you, so that you may rejoice in
God as your salvation. Has it been so with you,
dear one? Are you that favored singer? Are you
one of that chosen throng who can say, *"Thine
anger is turned away, and you comfortedst
me"*? Away with generalities. Do not be satisfied except with particulars. Little it matters to
you that Christ died for millions of men, if you
have no part in His death. Little blessing is it
to you that there should be joy from myriads of
pardoned hearts, if you should die unpardoned.
Seek a personal interest in Christ. Do not be
satisfied unless it has been satisfactorily revealed in your heart that your own sin has
been put away by an act of grace.

Remember that the word, *"thou,"* is spoken to those who have been brought into the
last degree of despair by sorrow. *"In that day
you shalt say, though thou wast angry with me,
thine anger is turned away."* You poor down-
trodden heart, where are you? Woman of sorrowful spirit, rejoice, for in that day of mercy
you will sing. Broken-hearted sinner, ready to
destroy yourself from anguish of conscience, in

the day of God's mercy, you will rejoice. Your note will be all the sweeter because you have had the most sin to be forgiven and felt most the anger of God burning in your soul. Dwell on that. May God grant that this is realized personally by all of us.

The next thing to be noted in the preliminaries is **the Teacher**. *"In that day you shalt say..."* Who says this? It is God alone who can so positively declare, *"thou shalt say."* Who but the Lord can thus command man's heart and speech? It is the Lord alone. He who has made us is Master of our spirits. By His omnipotence He rules in the world of mind as well as matter, and all things happen as He ordains. He states, *"In that day,* [that is, in God's own time] *thou shalt say,"* and He who so declares will make good the word. Here is revealed God's will. What the Lord wills shall be accomplished, and what He declares will be spoken assuredly shall be spoken.

Here is consolation to those feeble folk who fear the word will not be fulfilled in them. *"Thou shalt say,"* is a divine word and cannot fail. The Lord alone can give a man the right to say, *"Thine anger is turned away."* If any man presumes to say, "God has turned His anger from me," without a warrant from the Most High, he lies to his own confusion. However, when it is written, *"Thou shalt say,"* God has said, "I will make it true, so that you will be fully justified in the declaration."

Yet more comfort is found here, for even when the right to such a blessing is bestowed, we are often unable to enjoy it because of weakness. Unbelief is frequently so great that many things which are true we cannot receive. Under a sense of sin we are so despondent that we think God's mercy too great for us. Therefore we are not able to appropriate the blessing presented to us, though it be inexpressibly delightful. Blessed be God, the Holy Ghost knows how to chase away our unbelief and give us power to embrace the blessing. He can make us accept the covenant favor and rejoice in it, so as to declare the joy.

I have tried to induce many to believe comfortable truths about themselves, but they have fairly defeated me. I have put the Gospel plainly to them, feeling sure that its promises were meant for them, and have said within my heart, "Surely they will be comforted. Certainly their broken hearts will be bound up by that gracious word." But I cannot make anyone say, "Lord, I will praise You." I am unable to lead them to faith and peace.

However, my joy is that my Master can do what His servant cannot. He can make the tongue of the dumb sing. He delights to look after desperate cases. Man's impossibility becomes His opportunity. Where the most affectionate words of people fail, the consolations of the blessed Spirit are divinely efficacious. He does not merely bring oil and wine, but He

97

knows how to pour them into wounds and heal the anguish of contrite spirits. I pray that the Master, who alone can teach us to sing this song, may graciously instruct those who have been seeking rest, but finding none. *"I am the LORD thy God which teacheth thee to profit"* (Isaiah 48:17). He can put a song in your heart, for nothing is beyond the range of His grace.

Notice another preliminary, namely, **the tone of the song**. *"Thou shalt say, O Lord, I will praise thee."* The song is to be an open one, avowed, vocally uttered, heard by men, and published abroad. It is not to be a silent feeling, the kind of soft music whose sweetness is spent within the spirit. Rather in that day you will say, you will speak it forth, you will testify and bear witness to what the Lord has done for you. When a man gets his sins forgiven, he cannot help revealing the secret. *"When the Lord turned again the captivity of Zion, we were like them that dream. Then was our mouth filled with laughter, and our tongue with singing"* (Psalm 126:1-2). Even if the forgiven one cannot speak with his tongue, he can say it with his eye. His countenance, his manner, his very gait will betray him. The gracious secret must ooze out in some fashion. Spiritual men, at any rate, will find it out, and with thankfulness mark the joyful evidences.

I know that, before I found the Savior, had you known me, you would have observed my solitary habits. If you had followed me to my bed chamber, to my Bible, and to my knees, you would have heard groans and sighs which revealed a sorrowful spirit. Ordinary amusements of youth had few attractions for me then. Conversation, however cheerful, yielded me no comfort. But the very morning that I really heard the Gospel message, *"Look unto me, and be ye saved, all the ends of the earth"* (Isaiah 45:22), I am certain that no person who knew me could have helped remarking the difference even in my face. A change came over my spirit, which as I remember was even indicated in the way I walked, for the heavy step of melancholy was exchanged for a more cheerful pace. The spiritual condition affects the bodily state, and it was evidently so with me. My delight at being forgiven was no ordinary sensation. I could have fairly leaped for joy.

"All through the night I wept full sore
    But morning brought relief;
That hand which broke my bones before,
    Then broke my bonds of grief.

"My mourning he to dancing turns,
    For sackcloth joy he gives
A moment, Lord, thine anger burns
    But long thy favor lives."

If I had not declared my deliverance, the very stones must have cried out. It was not in my heart to keep it back, but I am sure I could not have done so if I had desired. God's grace does not come into the heart as a beggar into a barn and lie hidden away as if it stole a night's lodging. No, its arrival is known all over the house. Every chamber of the soul testifies to its presence. Grace is like a bunch of lavender: it discovers itself by its sweet smell. Like the nightingale, it is heard where it is not seen. Like a spark which falls into the midst of straw, it burns, blazes, and consumes until it reveals itself by its own energetic operations.

O soul, burdened with sin, if Christ comes to you and pardons you, I am certain that before long all your bones will say, *"Lord, who is like unto thee?"* (Psalm 35:10). You will be of the same mind as David when he cried, *"Deliver me from bloodguiltiness, O God, thou God of my salvation: and my tongue shall sing aloud of thy righteousness"* (Psalm 51:14). You will gladly say with him, *"Thy vows are upon me, O God: I will render praise unto thee, for thou have delivered my soul from death"* (Psalm 56:12-13). Not only will you soberly tell what great things grace has does for you, but more than likely your exuberant joy may lead you beyond the boundaries of solemn decorum.

The precise and slow going will condemn you, but you need not mind, for you can offer the same excuse for it as David made to Michal when he danced before the ark. Far be it from me to condemn you if you cry, "Hallelujah," or clap your hands. It is our cold custom to condemn every demonstration of feeling, but I am sure Scripture does not warrant us in our condemnation. We find such passages as these: *"O clap your hands, all ye people; shout unto God with the voice of triumph"* (Psalm 47:1). *"Praise him upon the loud cymbals: praise him upon the high sounding cymbals"* (Psalm 150:5). If the overflowing of holy joy seems to be disorderly, does it matter since God accepts it? He who gets his liberty from a long confinement in prison may well take a skip or two with an extra leap for joy. Who would begrudge him? He who has long been hungry and famished, when he sees the table spread, may be excused if he eats with more eagerness than politeness. Yes, they say, *"I will praise thee, O Lord."* In the very disorderliness of their demonstration, they more emphatically say, *"I will praise thee: though thou wast angry with me, thine anger is turned away."*

Now let us turn our attention to the song itself. Notice the fact that **all of the song concerns the Lord**. It is all addressed to Him. *"O Lord, I will praise thee: though thou wast angry, thine anger is turned away."* When a soul escapes from the bondage of sin and becomes consciously pardoned, it resembles the apostles on the Mount Tabor who saw no man except Jesus. While you are seeking grace, you think much of the minister, the service, the outward form; but the moment you find peace in God through the precious blood of Christ, you will think of your pardoning God only.

How small everything becomes in the presence of that dear cross, where God the Savior loved and died! When we think of all our iniquity being cast into the depths of the sea, we can no more boast of anything that was once our glory. The instrumentality by which peace came to us will be always dear to us. We esteem the preacher of the Gospel who presented salvation to us as our spiritual father, but still we would never think of praising him. We will give all the glory to our God. As for each of us personally, self will sink like lead amid the waters when we find Christ. God will be all in all when iniquity is pardoned.

I have often thought that if some of my fellow pastors, who preach a Gospel in which there is little of the grace of God, had felt a little more conviction of sin in being converted, they would be sure to preach a clearer and more gracious Gospel. Now many appear to leap into peace without any conviction of sin. They do not seem to have known what the guilt of sin means, but they scramble into peace before the burden of sin has been felt. It is not for me to judge, but I must confess I have my fears of those who have never felt the terrors of the Lord. I look upon conviction of sin as a good ground work for a well-instructed Christian. I observe as a rule that when a man has been put in the prison of the law, made to wear the heavy chains of conviction, and at last obtains his liberty through the precious blood, he is sure to proclaim the grace of God and magnify divine mercy. He feels that in his case salvation must be of grace from first to last, and magnifies most the grace of God.

Those who have not experienced the anger of God over their sinfulness, whose conversion has been of the easy kind, produced more from excitement than by depth of thought, seem to me to choose a flimsy divinity in which man is more prominent and God is less regarded. I am sure of this one thing, that I personally desire to ascribe conversion in my own case entirely to the grace of God and to give God all the glory for it. I dread any conversion which in any way may deprive God of being, by His everlasting word, the cause of it; by the effectual sacrifice of His Son, the direct agent of it; and by His continued working through the Holy Ghost, the perfecter of it. Give God all the praise. You must do so, if you have thoroughly experienced the weight of God's anger and what the turning away of it means.

The next thing in this song is, that it includes **repentant memories**. *"O Lord, I will praise thee: though thou wast angry with me."* There was a time when we were conscious that God was angry with us. When was that, and how did we know that God was angry with us? Outsiders think that when we talk about conversion we are merely talking sentimental theories, but let me assure you that it is as much matter of fact to us with regard to our spiritual nature as feelings of sickness and of recovery are real and actual.

As some of us read the Word of God, believing it to be an inspired book, we perceived that it contained a law, holy and just, the breach of which was threatened with eternal death. As we read it, we discovered that we had broken that law, not in some points, but in all. We were obliged to feel that all the sentences of that book against sinners were sentences against us. Perhaps we had read these chapters before, but we gave them no serious thought until on one occasion we were led to see that we stood condemned by the law of God as contained in holy Scripture. Then we knew that God was angry with us. It was not a mere idea of our own conjecture: we had this Book as evidence of it. If that Book were indeed true, we knew we were condemned. We dared not try to convince ourselves that the old Book was a cunningly-devised fable; we knew it was not. Therefore, from its testimony, we concluded that God was angry with us.

At the same time we learned this terrible truth from the Book, our conscience suddenly awoke and confirmed the fact. It said, "What the Book declares is correct. The just God must be angry with such a sinful being as you are." Conscience brought to our recollection many things which we would have preferred to forget. It revealed to us the evil of our hearts which we had no wish to remember. As we looked at Scripture by the light of conscience, we concluded that we were in a very dreadful plight, because God was angry with us. Then there entered into us at the same time, above all the rest, a certain work of the Holy Spirit called conviction of sin, *"When he, the Spirit of truth is come...he shall reprove the world of sin"* (John 16:13, 8). He has come and convinced us of sin in a way in which the Scripture and conscience would not have done apart from Him. But His light shone in on us, and we felt as we never felt before. Sin appeared exceeding sinful, as it was committed against infinite love and goodness. Then it seemed as though hell must swallow us up and the wrath of God must devour us. Oh, the trembling and the fear, the dismay and the alarm which then possessed our spirits! Yet now, the remembrance of it is cause for thankfulness.

In the Hebrew, the wording of our text is slightly different from what we get in the English. Our English translators have very wisely put in the word *"though,"* a little earlier than it occurs in the Hebrew. The Hebrew would run something like this, "O Lord, I will praise thee; thou wast angry with me." Now we can praise God that He made us feel His anger. You ask, "Is a sense of anger cause for praise?" No, not if it remains alone, but because it drives us to Christ. If wrath had been laid up for us hereafter, it would be a cause of horror, deep and dreadful. However, because it was let loose in a small measure upon us here, we were thus condemned in conscience so that we might not be condemned at the last. Therefore, we have reason for much thankfulness.

We would never have felt His love if we had not felt His anger. We laid hold on His mercy because of necessity. No soul will accept Christ Jesus until it must. It is not driven to faith until it is driven to self-despair. God's angry face makes Christ's loving face dear to us. We could never look at the Christ of God, unless first of all the God of Christ had looked at us through the tempest and made us afraid. "I will praise You, that You let me feel Your anger, in order that I might be driven to discover how that anger could be turned away." So you see, the song in its deep bass note includes plaintive recollections of sin pressing heavily on the spirit.

The song of our text contains **blessed certainties**. *"I will praise thee; though thou wast angry with me, thine anger is turned away."* Can a man know that and be quite sure that he is forgiven? Yes, he can. He can be as sure of pardon as he is of his existence, as infallibly certain as he is of a mathematical proposition. Someone asks, "How?" Surely, this is a matter for spiritual men, yet at the same time it is a matter of certainty as clearly as anything can be humanly ascertained.

The confidence of a man's being pardoned, and God's anger being turned away from him, is not based upon his merely feeling that it is so or his merely believing that it is so. You are not pardoned because you work yourself up into a comfortable frame of mind and think you are pardoned. That may be a delusion. You are not necessarily delivered from God's anger because you believe you are. You may be believing a lie, and may believe what you like, but that does not make it true. There must be a fact going before, and if that fact is not there, you may believe what you choose, but it is pure imagination, nothing more.

On what ground does a man know that God's anger is turned away? I answer this way: on the truth of the Bible. *"It is written"* (Matthew 4:4) is our basis of assurance. I turn to that Book and discover that Jesus Christ the Son of God came into this world and became the substitute for a certain body of men; that he took their sin and was punished in their stead in order that God, without the violation of His justice, might forgive as many as are washed in Christ's blood. My question then is, for whom did Christ die? The moment I turn to the Scriptures, I find very conspicuously on its page this declaration, that *"Jesus Christ came into the world to save sinners"* (1 Timothy 1:15). I am a sinner—of that I am certain—which gives me some hope. I next find that *"he that believeth on him is not condemned"* (John 3:18). Looking into myself, I find that I do really believe, that is, I trust Jesus. Very well, then I am sure I am not condemned, for God has declared I am not. I read again, *"He that believeth and is baptized shall be saved"* (Mark 16:16). I know that I have believed. I trust my salvation with Christ and have, in obedience to His command, been baptized. Then I am saved and will be saved, for the Word says so.

Assurance is simply a matter of testimony which we receive. He that believes in Christ receives the testimony of God, and that is the only testimony he needs. I know it has been thought that you get some special revelation in your own soul, some flash as it were of light, some extraordinary intimation, but nothing of the kind is absolutely necessary. I know that *"the Spirit itself beareth witness with our spirits, that we are the children of God"* (Romans 8:16), but the first essential matter is God's witness in the Word. *"He that believeth not God, hath made him a liar; because he believeth not the record that God gave of his Son"* (1 John 5:10). God's witness concerning His Son is that if you trust His Son, you are saved. His Son suffered for you. His Son bore the punishment that was due you for your sins. God declares that you are forgiven for Christ's sake. He cannot punish twice for offenses, first His Son and then you. He cannot demand retribution from His law to vindicate His justice, first from your Substitute and then from you.

Was Christ your substitute? That is the question. He was if you trust Him. Trusting

Him is the evidence that He was a substitute for you. Now see then that the moment have come to trust my soul forever in the hands of Christ, God's anger is turned away from me because it was turned upon Christ. I stand, guilty sinner as I am in myself, absolved before God. None can lay anything to my charge, for my sins were laid on Christ and punished through Christ, and I am clear. Now, what will I say to the Lord but, *"I will praise thee, for though thou wast angry with me, thine anger is turned away, and thou comfortedst me."* It is a matter of certainty. It is not a matter of "ifs," "ands," or "buts," but of fact. At this moment you are either forgiven or you are not; you are either clean in God's sight or else the wrath of God abides on you. I urge you, do not rest until you know which it is. If you find out that you are unforgiven, seek the Savior. *"Believe in the Lord Jesus Christ, and thou shalt be saved"* (Acts 16:31). But if you believe in Him, you are no longer guilty—you are forgiven. Do not sit down and fret as if you were guilty, but enjoy the liberty of the children of God. *"Therefore being justified by faith, we have peace with God through our Lord Jesus Christ"* (Romans 5:1).

I must add that our song includes **holy resolutions**: *"I will praise thee."* I will do it with my heart in secret. I will get alone and make my expressive silent hymn His praise. I will sit and pour out liquid songs in tears of gratitude, welling up from my heart. I will

praise Him in the church of God. I will search
out other believers, and I will tell them what
God has done for me. I will cast in my lot with
His people: if they are despised, I will bear the
shame with them and count it honor. I will
unite myself to them and help them in their
service. If I can magnify Christ by my testimony among them, I will do it. I will praise
Him in my life. I will make my business praise
Him. I will make my parlor and my drawing
room, my kitchen and my field praise Him. I
will not be content unless all I am and all I
have praises Him. I will make a harp of the
whole universe. I will make earth and heaven,
space and time to be strings on which my joyful fingers play lofty tunes of thankfulness. I
will praise my God. My heart is fixed. I will
sing and give praise. When I die—or rather
pass from this life to another—I, who have
been forgiven so much sin through such a
Savior, will continue to praise Him.

> "Oh, how I long to join the choir
>   Who worship at his feet!
> Lord, grant me soon my heart's desire!
>   Soon, soon thy work complete!"

Note that this is a song which is **peculiar
in its character** and appropriate only to the
people of God. I may say of it, "No man could
learn this song but the redeemed." Only he
who has felt his own vileness and has had it

washed away in the "fountain filled with blood," can know its sweetness. It is not a Pharisee's song: it has no likeness to *"God, I thank thee that I am not as other men"* (Luke 18:11). Rather, it confesses, *"Thou wast angry with me,"* admitting that the singer was just like others, but it glories that through infinite mercy, the divine anger is turned away. Here it leans on the Savior. It is not a Sadducean song: doubting does not mingle with the lyrics. It is not the philosopher's query, "There may be a God, or there may not be." It is the voice of a believing worshipper. It is not, "I may or may not be guilty." Every note of it is positive. I know and feel that *"thou wast angry with me,"* yet I am sure too that *"thine anger is turned away."* I believe it by the witness of God, and I cannot doubt His Word.

It is a song of strong faith and of humility. Its spirit is a precious incense made up of many costly ingredients. We have here not only one characteristic, but **many rare virtues**. **Humility** confesses, *"Thou wast angry with me."* **Gratitude** sings, *"Thine anger is turned away."* **Patience** cries, *"You comfortedst me,"* while holy joy springs up and says, *"I will praise thee."* **Faith, hope, and love** all have their notes here; from the bass of humility to the highest soprano of glorious communion, all the different parts are represented. It is a full song, the symphonic swelling of the heart.

I conclude with some words on **the practical results** from the subject. One is a word of **consolation**, consolation to you who are under God's anger right now. My heart goes out to you. I know what your heartache is. I knew it for a period of five long years while I mourned the guilt and curse of sin. Poor soul, you are in a sad plight indeed, but be of good cheer. You have in your heart a key which will open every lock in the doubting castle in which you are now confined. If you but have the heart to take it out of your bosom and out of the Word of God, and use it, liberty is near. I will show you that key. Look at it: *"Him that cometh to me, I will in no wise cast out"* (John 6:37). "Oh, but that does not happen to fit," you say. Well, here's another: *"The blood of Jesus Christ his Son cleanseth from all sin"* (1 John 1:7). Does not that meet your case? Then let me try again: *"He is able also to save them to the uttermost that come unto God by him"* (Hebrews 7:25). *"To the uttermost"*—dwell on that and be comforted. I never knew God to shut a soul in the prison of conviction, but that sooner or later He released the captive. The Lord will surely bring you out of that low dungeon. The worst thing in the world is to go unchastised. To be allowed to sin and eat honey with it is the precursor of damnation; but to sin and have the wormwood of repentance with it is the prelude of being saved. If the Lord has embittered your sin, He has designs of love

112

towards you. His anger will yet be turned away. *"When the poor and needy seek water, and there is none, and their tongue faileth for thirst, I the Lord will hear them, I the God of Israel will not forsake them"* (Isaiah 41:17).

The next is a word of **admonition**. Some of you hare been forgiven, but are you praising God as you should? I have heard say, that in our churches there are not more than five percent who are doing any real work for Christ. I would be very sorry if that were true of the church I pastor, but I fear there are more than five percent who are doing nothing. Where are you who have felt His anger pass away, and yet are not praising Him? Come, stir yourself, and seek to serve Jesus. Do you not know that you are meant to be the winners of souls? The American beekeeper, when he wants to collect a hive, first catches a single bee, puts it in a box with a piece of honeycomb, and then shuts the door. After awhile, when the bee is well fed, he lets it out. It comes back again after more of the sweet, bringing companions with it. When they have eaten the honey, they always bring yet more bees. Thus eventually there is a goodly assembly for the hive.

In this same fashion you ought to act. If you have found mercy, you ought to praise God and tell others, so that they may believe and in their turn lead others to Jesus. This is the way the kingdom of God grows. I am afraid you are guilty here. See to it, dear ones, and who can tell of what use you yet may be? There was a dear servant of Christ who was just on the verge of the grave, very old and ill, frequently delirious. The doctors said no one must go into the chamber except the nurse. A little Sunday-school boy, who was rather curious, peeped in at the door to look at the minister. The poor dying servant of God saw him, and the ruling passion was strong even in death. He called him. "David," said he, "did you ever close in with Christ? I have done so many a time, and I long that you may." Fifty years later, that boy was living and bearing testimony that the dying words of the good man had brought him to Jesus, for by them he was led to seek Christ.

You do not know what a word might do if you would but speak it. Do not keep back the good news that might bring salvation to your wife, to your husband, to your child, to your servant. If you have indeed felt the Lord's anger pass away from you, right now, on your knees repeat this vow, "My God, I will praise You! I have been a sluggard. I have been very silent about You. I am afraid I have not given You of my substance as I ought. I am sure I have not given You of my heart as I should. But oh, forgive the past, and accept your poor servant yet again. Then *'I will praise thee; for though thou wast angry with me, thine anger is turned away, and you comfortedst me.'*"

God bless you, for Christ's sake.

Chapter 5

Ethan's Song in the Night

"I will sing of the mercies of the Lord forever:
with my mouth will I make known
thy faithfulness to all generations.
For I have said, Mercy shall be built up forever:
thy faithfulness shalt thou establish
in the very heavens."
—Psalm 89:1-2

This psalm is one of the choicest songs in the night. Amid a stream of troubled thoughts, there stands an island of rescue and redemption which supplies standing room for wonder and worship, while the music of the words sounds sweetly in our ears like the murmuring of a river. Read the entire psalm carefully and it will arouse your sympathy, for the author was bearing bitter reproach and was almost broken-hearted by the grievous calamities of his nation. Yet his faith was strong in the faithfulness of God. So he sang of the stability of the divine covenant when the outlook of circumstances was dark and cheerless. Nor did he ever sing more sweetly than he sang in that night of his sorrow. Greatly does it glorify God for us to sing His high praises in storms of adversity and on beds of affliction. It magnifies His mercy if we can bless and adore Him when He takes as well as when He gives. It is good that out of the very mouth of the burning fiery furnace there should come a more burning note of grateful praise.

I am told that there is a great deal of relief from sorrow in complaining, that our murmuring may sometimes tend to relieve our pain. I suppose it is so. Certainly it is a good thing to weep, for I have heard it from the mouth of many witnesses. Most of us have felt that there are griefs too deep for tears, and that a flood of tears proves the sorrow has begun to abate.

However, I think the best relief for sorrow is to sing. This man tried it, at any rate. When mercy seems to have departed, it is well to sing of departed mercy. When no present blessing appears, it is a present blessing to remember the blessings of past years and to rehearse the praises of God for all His former mercies towards us. Two sorts of songs we ought to keep up, even if the present appears to yield us no theme: **the song of the past** for what God has done, and **the song of the future** for the grace we have not tasted yet—the covenant blessings held in the pierced hand, safe and sure against the time to come.

Beloved, I want you to feel the spirit of gratitude within your heart. Even though your mind may be heavy, your countenance sad, and your circumstances gloomy, still let the generous impulse kindle and glow. Come, let us sing unto the Lord. It is not much for us to sing God's praises in fair weather. The shouts of "harvest home" over the loaded hay wagon are proper, but they are only natural. Who would not sing then? What bird is silent when the sun is rising and the dews of spring are sparkling? But the choicest choir charms the stars of night, and no note is sweeter, even to the human ear, than that which comes from the bare bough amid the snows of dark winter. Sorrowful ones, your hearts are tuned to notes the joyful cannot reach. Yours is the full range of tone and volume. You are harps on which the chief Player of stringed instruments can display His matchless skill to a larger degree than on the unafflicted. May He do so now.

Some will not readily yield in this holy exercise. Like Elijah, we will try to run before the king's chariot in the matter of praise. Accounting ourselves the greatest debtors of all to the grace and mercy of God, we must and will sing loudest of the crowd and make even:

"Heaven's resounding arches ring
    With shouts of sovereign grace."

I invite your attention to two things. First, we will look at the **work of the eternal Builder**: *"Mercy shall be built up forever."* Secondly, we will listen to **the resolve of an everlasting singer**: *"I will sing of the mercies of the Lord forever."* For the best handling of the subject, I will discuss the second verse first. In the book of common prayer, the canon prescribes that a certain form of words is "to be said or sung." From the text we are to do both. The second verse begins *"I have said,"* and then the first verse begins *"I will sing."* We will say and sing, too. God grant we may say it in the depth of our hearts, and afterwards that our mouths may sing it and make it known unto all generations.

First, let us contemplate the eternal Builder and His wonderful work. *"I have said, Mercy shall be built up forever: thy faithfulness shalt thou establish in the very heavens."* I can see a vast mass of ruins. Heaps upon heaps lie around me. A stately edifice has tumbled down. Some terrible disaster has occurred. There it lies—cornice, pillar, pinnacle, everything of ornament and of utility, broken, scattered, dislocated. The world is strewn with the debris. Journey wherever you will, the desolation is before your eyes. Who has done this? Who has cast down this temple? What hand has ruined this magnificent structure? Manhood has been destroyed, and sin was the agent that effected the fall. It is man broken by his

118

sin. Iniquity has done it. Oh, devastation, what destruction have you wrought in the earth! What desolation you have made unto the ends of the world! Everywhere is ruin. Futile attempts are made to rebuild this temple upon its own heap. The Babel tower arises out of the rubbish and abides for a season, but it is soon broken down. The mountain of decay and corruption becomes even more hopeless of restoration. All that man has done with his greatest effort is but to make a huge display of his total failure to recover his position, to realize his ostentatious plans, or to restore his own fleeting memories of better things. They may build; they may pile stone upon stone and cement them together with mortar. However, their rude structure will all crumble to dust again, for the first ruin will be perpetuated even to the end. So must it be, because sin destroys all. I am vexed in my spirit and very troubled as I look at these ruins, fit habitations for the bittern and the dragon, the mole and the bat. Alas, that manhood should be thus destroyed!

But what else do I see? I behold the great original Builder coming forth from the ivory palaces to undo this mischief. He comes not with implements of destruction to cast down every vestige, but He advances with plummet and line so that He may set up and establish on a sure foundation a noble pile that will not crumble with time, but endure throughout all ages. He comes forth with mercy.

Thus I said as I saw the vision, *"Mercy shall be built up forever."* There was **no material but mercy** with which a temple could be constructed among men. What can meet the guilt of human crimes but mercy? What can redress the misery occasioned by wanton transgression but mercy? Mere kindness could not do it. Power alone—even omnipotence—could not accomplish it. Wisdom could not even commence until mercy stood at her right hand. But when I saw mercy intervene, I understood the meaning. Something was to be done that would change the dreary picture that made my heart groan. At the advent of mercy, the walls would soon rise until the roof ascended high and the palace received within its renovated glory the sublime Architect who erected it. I knew that now there would be songs instead of sighs, since God had come, and come in mercy.

Blessed was that day when mercy, God's Benjamin, His last-born attribute, appeared. Surely it was the son of our sorrow, but it was also the son of His right hand. There would have been no need for mercy if it had not been for our sin. From direst evil the Lord displayed the greatest good. When mercy came—God's darling, for He said, *"he delighteth in mercy"* (Micah 7:18)—then was there hope that the ruins of the fall would no longer be the perpetual misery of men. *"Mercy shall be built up."*

If you closely scan the passage, you will clearly perceive that the psalmist has the idea

of **God's mercy being manifest in building**, because a great breach has to be repaired
and the ruins of mankind are to be restored. As
for building, it is a very **substantial** operation. A building is something which is palpable
and tangible to our senses. We may have plans
and schemes which are only visionary, but
when it comes to building, as those who have
to build know, there is something real being
done—something more than surveying the
ground and drawing the plans. What real work
God has done for men! What real work in the
gift of His dear Son! The product of His infinite purpose now becomes evident. He is
working out His great designs after the counsel
of His own will. What real work there is in the
regeneration of His people. That is no fiction.
Mercy is built, and the blessings that you and I
have received have not mocked us. They have
not been the dream of fanatics nor the fancy of
enthusiasts. God has done real work for you
and for me, as we can testify.

"For I have said, Mercy shall be built."
That is no sham, no dream; it is the act and
deed of God. Mercy has been built. A thing
that is built is a **fixed** thing. It exists—exists
really, and exists according to a substantial
plan. It is presumed to be permanent. True, all
earthly structures will eventually deteriorate
and decay, and man's buildings will dissolve in
the last great fire. Still, a building is much
more durable than a tent. *"I have said, Mercy*

121

shall be built." It is not a movable berth, but a fixed habitation! I have found it so, have you? Some of you began to perceive God's mercy many years ago when heads that are now bald or gray had locks bushy and black as a raven, when you were curly-headed boys and girls that clambered on your father's knee. You remember the mercy of your God, and it has continued with you—a fixed, substantial, real thing. Your old family house has not been more fixed than the mercy of God. There has been a warm place for you by the fireside from your childhood until now, and a mother's love has not failed. But more substantial than a house has been the mercy of God to you. You can endorse the declaration of Ethan: *"I have said, Mercy shall be built."*

A building is an **orderly** thing as well as a fixed thing. There is a scheme and **design** about it. *"Mercy shall be built."* God has gone about blessing us with designs that only His own infinite perfection could have completed. We have not seen the design yet in the full proportion. We will be lost in wonder, love, and praise when we see it all carried out. Now, however, we can already perceive some lines, some distinct traces of a grand design.

As I caught first one thought of God and then another, I said of His mercy toward me, *"Mercy shall be built."* I see that it definitely will be. This is no load of bricks. It is polished stones built one upon another. God's grace and goodness toward me have not come to me by chance, or as the blind distribution of a God who cared for all alike, and for none with any special purpose. No, there has been as much a specialty of purpose for me as if I were the only one He loved, though, praise His name, He has blessed and is blessing multitudes of others beside me. As I discovered that in His dealings of mercy there was a plan, I said, *"Mercy shall be built,"* and so it has been.

If I had the space, I would like to picture for you the digging of that foundation of mercy in past times, the marking out of the lines of mercy in the predestining purpose and the ancient covenant of God. I would appeal to your experience and entreat you to observe how progressively, line upon line, the many promises have been verified to you up until now. With what alacrity you would say, "Yes, the figure may run on all fours, if it likes, and may go on as many legs as a centipede. Yet there will be no spoiling of it; the metaphor is so good. Mercy has been in the course of construction and is now being built." So the song begins, *"Mercy shall be built."*

Notice now that the psalmist says, *"Mercy shall be built up."* Will you try to think for a minute upon these words, ***"built up"***? It is not merely a long, low wall of mercy that is formed to make an enclosure or to define a boundary, but a magnificent pile of mercy, whose lofty heights will draw admiring gazes, that is being built up. God piles mercy on top of mercy. He gives one favor so that we may receive another.

There are some covenant blessings that you and I are not ready to receive yet. They would not be suitable to our present capacities. *"I have yet many things to say unto you, but ye cannot bear them now"* (John 16:12). Weak eyes that are gradually recovering their use must not have too much light. A man half-starved must not be fed at once upon substantial meat: he must have the nutriment gently administered to him. An excess of rain might inundate the land and wash up the plants, while gentle showers refresh the thirsty soil and invigorate the vegetation.

Likewise, **mercy is bestowed on us in measure**. God does not give us every spiritual blessing at once. There are the blessings of our childhood in grace, which we perhaps will not so much enjoy when we come to be strong men. Just so, the blessings of the strong man and of the father would crush the child. God abounds toward us in all wisdom and prudence in distributing His gifts. I said, "Yes, *'Mercy shall be built up.'* There will be one mercy on another."

If I only had a vivid imagination and a tongue gifted with eloquence, then I would try to portray the twelve courses of the new Jerusalem and show how the stones of fair colors came one next to the other, so that the colors set each other off and blended into a wondrous harmony. I can clearly see that the mercy of the azure will not come first, but there will be the mercy of the emerald underneath it. There will be a progression made in the preciousness of the stones with which God will build us up. We cannot tell what the next is to be; certainly not what the next after that is to be, nor the next after that. But as I saw half-a-dozen of the courses of God's mercy, I said, *"Mercy shall be built up."* As I see it rising tier on tier, course on course, it gathers wonders. The longer I gaze, the more I am lost in contemplation. Silent with astonishment, spell-bound with the fascinating vision, I think, I believe, and I know that *"Mercy shall be built up."*

Further, **mercy awakens expectations**. I am waiting eagerly for the next scene. The designs of mercy are not exhausted. The deeds of mercy are not all told. The display of mercy must reach higher than has ever yet dawned upon my imagination. Its foundations were laid deep. In great mercy He gave me a broken heart. That was pure mercy, for God accepts broken hearts. They are very precious in His sight. But it was a greater mercy when He gave me a new heart which was wrapped up in His love and filled with His joy. Let us remember how He showed us the evil of sin and caused us to feel a sense of shame. That was a choice mercy, but it was a clearer mercy when He gave us a sense of pardon. It was a blessed day when He gave us the little faith that tremblingly touched His garment's hem. It was

125

better when He gave us faith as a grain of mustard seed that grew. It has been better still when by faith we have been able to do mighty works for Him. We know not what we will do in the future when He gives us more faith.

Far less can we imagine how our powers will develop in heaven, where faith will come to its full perfection. It will not die, as some idly pretend. There we will implicitly believe in God. With the place of His throne as the point of our survey, we will see nothing but His sovereign will to shape events. Thus, with joyful assurance of hope, we will look onward to the advent of our Lord Jesus Christ and the glory that is to follow. We will sit in heaven and sing that the Lord reigns. We will gaze on the earth and behold how it trembles at the coming of the King of Kings. With radiant faces we will smile at Satan's rage. We do not know what any one of our graces may be built up into, but if you are conscious of any growth in any grace, you have learned enough to appreciate the voice that speaks in this manner, *"I have said, Mercy shall be built up forever."*

Once again read this verse with very great emphasis. Notice how it rebukes the proud and the haughty, and how it encourages the meek and lowly in spirit. *"I have said, Mercy shall be built up forever."* In the edification of the saints, there is nothing else but mercy.

Some people seem to imagine that when we get to a certain point in grace, we do not need to **petition for mercy**. Dear ones, if any of you get into the frame of mind in which you believe that you need not make any confession of sin nor ask pardon of sin, you are trifling with the very truths of which you seem to hold dear. I do not care what doctrine it is that brings you to that point. You are in a danger-ous state if you stay there. Get back to the truth quickly. Your right position is at the throne of grace, and a throne of grace is meant for people that want grace. You need grace now, more than ever. Without mercies new every morning, as the manna that fed the Is-raelites of old, your days will be full of misery.

Your Lord and Master taught you to say not only *"Our Father which art in heaven"* and *"Thy kingdom come,"* but He instructed you constantly to pray, *"Forgive us our trespasses as we forgive them that trespass against us"* (Matthew 6:9, 10, 12). "But I have no tres-passes," someone says. Dear one, look at your own heart. I will have no argument with you. Take the bandage off your eyes. You are about as full of sin as an egg is full of protein. Among the rest of your many sins is this rotten egg of an accursed pride about your own state of heart. Whatever you say, *"I said, Mercy shall be built up forever."*

I expect God to deal with me on the basis of mercy as long as I live. I do not expect that He will build me up in any way but according to His grace, compassion, and forgiving love. If there are any creatures in this world that can boast of having progressed beyond the need of asking for mercy, I have not learned their secret of self-deception. I do know of some professors of the faith who climb so high up the ladder that they come down the other side. It is very much like the wonderful growing in perfection of which they talk so foolishly. Often it means climbing so high that they are pure saints in their own estimation, but before long they have sunk so low that they are poor lost sheep in the eyes of the church. God grant that you may not fall by any such delusion.

"I have said, Mercy shall be built up forever." If we get to the gate of heaven and stand at the alabaster doorstep with our finger on the glittering latch, unless the mercy of God carries us over the threshold, we will be dragged down to hell even from the gates of paradise. Mercy, mercy, mercy! *"His mercy endureth forever"* (Psalm 118:1) because we always need it. As long as we are in this world, we will have to make our appeal to mercy and cry, "Father, I have sinned. Blot out my transgressions." That is, as I have said, what the text declares, *"I have said, Mercy shall be built up,"* and nothing else but mercy. There will not come a point when the angelic masons will stop and say, "Now then, the next course is to be merit. So far it has been mercy, but the next course is to be perfection in the flesh. The next course is to be no need of mercy." Absolutely

not! Mercy only, until the topstone is brought forth with shouts of *"Grace, grace unto it"* (Zechariah 4:7). *"Mercy shall be built up."*

Further cast your eyes on the Scripture. *"I said, mercy shall be built up forever."* Forever? Well, I have been peering back into the past, and I discover that nothing else but mercy can account for my being or my well-being. By the grace of God, I am what I am. The psalm of my life, though filled with varied stanzas, has but one chorus, *"His mercy endureth forever."* Will you look back, beloved, on all the building of your life and character? Any of it that has been real building—gold and silver and precious stones—has all been mercy, and so the building will go on. The operation is proceeding slowly but surely. Even though at this present hour you may be in grievous trouble, mercy is being built up for you. "Oh, no," say you, "I am tottering, my days are declining, and I feel I will be utterly cast down." Yes, you may be very conscious of your own weakness and infirmity; but the mercy of the Lord is steadfast, its foundation abides firm, not a single stone can be moved from its setting. The work is going on, storm or tempest notwithstanding.

Nothing is precarious about the fact that *"mercy shall be built up forever."* Let not the murky atmosphere that surrounds you blind the eyes of your understanding to this glorious word *"forever."* Rather, realize that if you are well set in this fabric of mercy, your castings down are often the way in which God builds up His mercy. You will be built up forever by His mercy. And if it goes on being built up forever—I am ravished with the thought, though I cannot give expression to it—what will it grow to? If it is going to be built up in the case of any one of you, for seventy years or so, it will be a grand pinnacle, an everlasting monument to the eternal Builder's praise. But you see it will continue, for it will be built up forever. What! Never cease? No, never. But will it ever come to a pause? No, *"mercy shall be built up forever."* It will go on towering upward. Do you imagine that eventually it will slow down? That is not likely. It is not God's way. He generally hastens His speed as He ripens His purposes.

I suspect that God will go on building up His mercy tier on tier forever. Someone asks, "Will its colossal altitude pierce the clouds and rise above the clear azure of the sky?" It will. Read the text: *"Thy faithfulness shalt thou establish in the very heavens"*—not in the heavens only, but in the *"very heavens,"* the heaven of heavens. **He will continue building you up in mercy**, dear brother or sister, until He gets you to heaven. He will build you up until He makes a heavenly man of you; until where Christ is, you are; and what Christ is, as far as He is man, you are also. With God Himself you will be allied, a child of God, an heir of heaven, a joint heir with Jesus Christ.

Again I wish I had an imagination, bold and clear, uncramped by all ideas built up by men, free to expand, and still able to cry, "Excelsior." Palaces, I think, are paltry, and castles and cathedrals are only grand in comparison with the little cottages that nestle on the plain. Even mountains, high as the Himalayan range or broad as the Andes, though their peaks are very lofty from our perspective, are mere specks on the surface of the great globe itself. Our earth is small among the celestial orbs, a little sister of the larger planets.

Figures quite fail me: my description must take another turn. I try and try again to realize the gradual rising of this temple of mercy which will be built up forever. Within the limits of my feeble vision, I can discern that it has risen above death, above sin, above fear, above all danger. It has risen above the terrors of the judgment day. It has out-soared the wreck of matter and the crash of worlds. It towers above all our thoughts. Our bliss ascends above angels' enjoyments. They have pleasures that were never checked by a pang of guilt, but they do not know the indescribable delight of free grace and undying love. It has ascended above all that I dare to speak of, for even the little I know has about it the idea that it is not lawful for a man to utter. It is built up into the very arms of Christ, where His saints will lie in paradise forever. *"I said, Mercy shall be built up forever."* **The building-up process will go on throughout eternity**.

Further, **what is once built will never fall down,** in whole or in part. That is the mercy of it. God is such a Builder that He finishes what He begins, and what He accomplishes is forever. *"The gifts and calling of God are without repentance"* (Romans 11:29). He does not do and undo, or build for His people after a covenant fashion and then cast down again because the counsel of His heart has changed. So let us sing and praise and bless the name of the Lord. I do hope that, from what our experience has taught us already, we are prepared to cry, like the psalmist, *"I have said, Mercy shall be built up forever: thy faithfulness shalt thou establish in the very heavens."*

Now let us examine the first verse. There are first that shall be last, and last that shall be first; so is it with our text. We have looked at the eternal Builder, let us listen to an everlasting singer. *"I will sing of the mercies of the Lord forever: with my mouth will I make known thy faithfulness to all generations."*

Here is a good and **godly resolution**: *"I will sing."* The singing of the heart is intended, and the singing of the voice is expressed, for the psalmist mentions his mouth. Equally true is it that the singing of his pen is implied, since the psalms that he wrote were for others to sing in generations that should follow. He says, *"I will sing."* I do not know what else he could do. God is building with mercy. We cannot assist Him in that. We have no mercy to contribute, and what is built is to be all of mercy. We cannot impart anything to the great temple which He is building. However, we can sit down and sing. It seems delightful that there should be no sound of hammer or noise of ax; that there should be no other sound than the voice of song, as when the ancient fabled instrument player was said to have built temples by the force of song. So will God build up His church, and so will He build us as living stones into the sacred structure. So will we sit and muse on His mercy until the music breaks forth from our mouths as we rise to stand and sing about it. I will sing of the mercy while the mercy is being built up. *"I will sing of the mercies of the Lord."*

But will not the psalmist soon quit these sweet notes and relapse into silence? No, he says, *"I will sing of the mercies of the Lord forever."* Will he not grow weary and wish for some other occupation? No, for true praise is a thirsty thing: when it drinks from a golden chalice, it soon empties it and yearns for deeper draughts with strong desire. It could drink up Jordan at a gulp. Singing praise to God is **a spiritual passion**. The saved soul delights itself in the Lord and sings on and on tirelessly. *"I will sing...forever,"* says he. Not, "I will get others to perform and then I will retire from the service," but rather, "I will myself sing. My own voice will take the solo, whoever may refuse to join in the chorus. I will sing, and with my mouth will I make known His faithfulness."

That is blessed—that singing personally and individually. It is a blessed thing to be one of a choir in the praise of God, and we like to have others with us in this happy employment. Yet, for all that, Psalm 103 is a most beautiful solo. It begins, *"Bless the Lord, O my soul,"* and it finishes up with *"Bless the Lord, O my soul."* There must be personal, singular praise for we have received personal, singular mercies. I will sing, *"I will sing of the mercies of the Lord forever."*

Now note the **subject** of his song: *"I will sing of the mercies of the Lord."* What, not of anything else? Are the **mercies of the Lord** his exclusive theme? *Arma virumque cano—* "Arms and the man, I sing," says the Latin poet. "Mercies and my God, I sing," says the Hebrew lyricist. "I will sing of mercies," says the devout Christian. If a man drinks from this fountain of mercy, he will sing far better than he who drinks of the Castalian fountain and on Parnassus begins to tune his harp.

> "Praise the mount, oh, fix me on it,
>   Mount of God's unchanging love."

Here we are taught a melodious sonnet, "sung by flaming tongues above." "I will sing of mercies, I will sing of mercies forever," he says, and I suppose the reason is because he knew God's mercies would be built up forever. The morning stars sang together when God's work of creation was completed. Suppose God created a world every day. Surely the morning stars would sing every day. God gives us a world of mercies every day: therefore, let us sing of His mercies forever. Any one day that you live, beloved, contains enough mercy to make you sing not only through that day but through the rest of your life. I have thought sometimes when I have received great mercies of God that I almost wanted to stop, rest, and be thankful, and say to Him, "My blessed Lord, do not send me anything more for a little while. I really must take stock of these. Come, my good secretaries, take down notes and keep a record of all His mercies."

Let us gratefully respond for the manifold gifts we have received and return our heartiest praise to God who is the giver of every good thing. But, dear me, before I can put the basketfuls of present mercies away on the shelf, there come wagons loaded with more mercy. What am I to do then, but to sit on the top of the pile and sing for joy of heart? So let us lift each parcel, look at each label, store them in the cupboard, and say, "It is certainly full of mercy." As for me, I will go and sit before the Lord like David, and say, *"Who am I, O Lord God? and what is my house, that thou hast brought me hitherto?...And is this the manner of man, O Lord God?"* (2 Samuel 7:18-19). *"I will sing of the mercies of the Lord forever,"* because I will never reach the end of them.

As Addison put it, "Eternity's too short to utter all thy praise." You will never accomplish the simple task of acknowledgments, because there will be constantly more mercies coming. You will always be in arrears. In heaven itself you will never have praised God sufficiently. You will want to begin heaven over again and have another eternity, if such a thing could be, to praise Him for the fresh benefits that He bestows. *"For I have said, mercy shall be built up forever."* Therefore, *"I will sing of the mercies of the Lord forever."* What a spectacle it will be as you sit in heaven and watch God building up His mercies forever, or, if it be the case, wander over all the worlds that God has made. I suppose we may do that and yet still have heaven for our home. Heaven is everywhere to the heart that lives in God. What a wonderful sight it will be to see God going on building up His mercy.

We have not acquired an idea of **the grandeur of the plan of mercy**. The grandeur of His justice no thought can conceive, no words can paint. Although there have been expressions and metaphors used about the wrath to come which cannot be found in Scripture, and are not justified, yet I am persuaded that there is no exaggeration possible of the

136

inviolability of God's law, of the truthfulness of His threatening, of the terror of His indignation, or of the holiness of the Lord, a holiness that will compel universal homage.

Nevertheless, you must always take care that you **balance your thoughts**. In the requital of His wrath, there will be a revelation of His righteousness. No sentence of His majesty will ever cast a shadow over His mercy, and every enemy will be speechless before the equity of His award. They that hate Him will hide their faces from Him, In burning shame they will depart to perpetual banishment from His presence. Their condemnation will not dim the purity of His attributes. The glory of the redeemed will also reveal the righteousness of Jehovah, and His saints will be perfectly satisfied when they are conformed to His likeness. On the summit of the eternal hill, you will sit down and survey the built-up mercy city which is now in the course of construction. It lies four square: its height is the same as its breadth, ever towering, ever widening, ever coming to that divine completion which, nevertheless, it has already attained, in another sense. We know that God in His mercy will be all in all. *"I will sing of the mercy of the Lord forever,"* because I will see His mercy built up forever.

This singing of Ethan was intended to be **instructive**. How large a class did he want to teach? He intended to make known God's mercy **to all generations**. Dear me, if a man teaches one generation, is not that enough? Modern thought does not venture beyond a decade, and it gets tame and tasteless before half that tiny span of sensationalism has given it time to evaporate. But the echoes of truth are not so transient. They endure, and by means of the printing press we can teach generation after generation, leaving books behind us. This good man has bequeathed this psalm, which is teaching us now, perhaps more so than it taught any generation closer to him. Will you transmit blessed testimonies to your children's children? It should be your desire to do something in the present life that will live after you are gone. It is one proof to us of our immortality that we instinctively long for a sort of immortality here. Let us strive to get it, not by carving our names on some stone, or writing our epitaphs upon a pillar, as Absalom did when he had nothing else by which to commemorate himself. (See 2 Samuel 18:18.) Rather, let us get to work to do something which will be a testimony to the mercy of God, that others will see when we are gone. Ethan said, *"Mercy shall be built up forever,"* and he is still teaching us that blessed fact.

Suppose you cannot write and your sphere of influence is very narrow. Still you will go on singing of God's praise forever, and you will go on teaching generations yet to come. You Sunday-school teachers, you will be Sunday-school teachers forever. "Oh, no," you say, "I cannot put stock in that." Well, but you will. You know it will always be Sunday when you get to heaven. There will never be any other day there, but one everlasting Sabbath. Through you and by you will be made known to angels, principalities, and powers, the manifold wisdom of God.

I often think some of you old, experienced saints could better teach me than I can teach you. You will teach me by and by. When we are in glory we will all be able to tell one another something of God's mercy. Your view of it, you know, differs from mine, and mine from another's. You, my dear friend, see mercy from one perspective; but even though you two are one together, your spouse sees it from another point of view and detects another facet of it which your eye has never caught. So we will barter and exchange our knowledge in heaven, and trade together and grow richer in our knowledge of God there. *I have said, mercy shall be built up forever: thy faithfulness shalt thou establish in the very heavens.*

Then I said, *"I will sing of the mercies of the Lord forever: with my mouth will I make known thy faithfulness to all generations."* We will go on exalting in God's mercy as long as we have any being, and that will be forever and ever. When we have been in heaven millions of years, we will not desire any other subject to speak of but the mercy of our blessed God. We will find an audience with charmed ears to sit and listen to the matchless tale, and some that will ask us to tell it yet again. They will come to heaven as long as the world lasts, some from every generation. We will see them streaming in at the gates more numerously, I hope, as the years roll by, until the Lord returns. We will continue to tell to newcomers what the Lord has done for us. We never can cease it. The heavens are continually telling the glory of God, and every star declares His praise in wondrous diversity. Just as the stars differ from one another in the glory of God above, so the saints will forever tell the story which yet will remain untold—the love we knew, but which surpassed our knowledge; the grace of which we drank, but yet was deeper than our draughts; the bounty in which we swam until we seemed to lose ourselves in love; the favor which was greater than our utmost conceptions and rose above our most eager desires.

God bless you, beloved, and send you out singing:

"All that remains for me
    Is but to love and sing,
And wait until the angels come,
    To bear me to my King."

Chapter 6

Praise for the Gift of Gifts

"Thanks be unto God for his unspeakable gift."
—*2 Corinthians 9:16*

In the chapter from which the text is taken, Paul is stirring up the Christians at Corinth to be ready with liberal gifts for the poor saints at Jerusalem. He finishes by reminding them of a greater gift than any they could bring. By this one short word of praise, *"Thanks be unto God for his unspeakable gift,"* he sets all their hearts singing. Let men give as liberally as they may, you can always proclaim the value of their gift: you can appraise it and add up its worth. But God's gift is unspeakable, unreckonable. You cannot fully estimate the value of what God gives.

The Gospel is a **Gospel of giving and forgiving**. We may sum it up in those two words. Hence, when the true spirit of it works

141

upon the Christian, he forgives freely and also gives freely. The large heart of God breeds large hearts in men, and they who live upon His bounty are led by His Spirit to imitate that bounty, according to their power.

However, I am not going to say anything further right now on the subject of liberality. I must get to the text immediately, hoping that we may really drink in the spirit of it, and out of full hearts use the apostle's language with more intense meaning than ever as we read his words: *"Thanks be unto God for his unspeakable gift."* I will begin by showing that salvation is altogether the gift of God, and as such is to be received by us freely. Then I will try to show that this gift is unspeakable, and, thirdly, that for this gift thanks should be rendered to God. Though it is unspeakable, yet we should speak our praise of it.

We start with the thought that **salvation is totally the gift of God**. Paul said, *"Thanks be unto God for his unspeakable gift."* Over and over again, we have to proclaim that salvation is wholly of grace—not of works, nor of wages, but the gift of God's great bounty to undeserving men. Often as I have preached this truth, I must keep on doing so, as long as there are men in the world who are self-righteous, and as long as there are minds in the world so slow to grasp the meaning of the word *grace*—that is, "free favor"—and as long as there are memories that find it difficult to retain the idea of salvation being God's free gift.

Let us say, simply and plainly, that **salvation must come to us as a gift from God**, for salvation comes to us by the Lord Jesus, and what else could Jesus be? The essence of salvation is the gift of God's only-begotten Son to die for us, that we might live through Him. I think you will agree with me that it is inconceivable that men have ever merited God giving His only-begotten Son to them. To give Christ to us, in any sense, must have been an act of divine charity; but to give Him up to die on that cruel and bloody tree, to yield Him up as a sacrifice for sin, must be a free favor that surpasses the limits of human thought. It is not plausible that any man could deserve such love.

It is plain that if man's sins needed a sacrifice, he did not deserve that a sacrifice should be found for him. The fact of his need proves his lack of merit and his guiltiness. He deserves to die. He may be rescued by another dying for him, but he certainly cannot claim that the eternal God should take from His bosom His only-begotten, well-beloved Son and put Him to death. The more you look that thought in the face, the more you will reject the idea that, by any possible sorrow, or by any possible labor, or by any possible promise, a man could put himself into the position of deserving to have Christ to die for him. If Christ came to save sinners, it must have been as a gift, a free gift of God. The argument to me is conclusive.

Besides, over and over again in God's Word, we are told that **salvation is not of works**. Although there are many who cling to the notion of man's works as grounds for salvation, yet as long as this Book stands and there are eyes to read it, it will bear witness against the idea of human merit, and it will speak out plainly for the doctrine that men are saved by faith, and not by works. Not just once, but often, it is written, *"The just shall live by faith"* (Habakkuk 2:4; Romans 1:17; Galatians 3:11; Hebrews 10:38). Moreover, we are told, *"Therefore it is of faith, that it might be by grace"* (Romans 4:16). The choice of salvation by believing, rather than by works, is made by God purposefully so that He might show that grace is a gift. *"Now to him that worketh is the reward not reckoned of grace, but of debt: but to him that worketh not, but believeth on him that justifieth the ungodly, his faith is counted for righteousness"* (Romans 4:4-5).

Faith is that virtue, that grace, which is chosen to bring us salvation, because it **never takes any of the glory to itself**. Faith is simply the hand that takes. When the beggar receives alms, he does not bless the hand that takes, but blesses the hand that gives. Therefore we do not praise the faith that receives, but the God who gives the gift. Faith is the eye that sees. When we see an object, we delight in the object, rather than in the eye that sees it. Thus we glory in the salvation which God bestows, not in faith. Faith is appointed as the porter to open the gate of salvation, because that gate turns on the hinges of free grace.

Additionally, may we always remember that we cannot be saved by the merit of our own works, because **holy works are themselves a gift**, the work of the grace of God. If you have faith, joy, and hope, who gave them to you? These did not spring up spontaneously in your heart. They were sown there by the hand of love. If you have lived a godly life for years, if you have been a diligent servant of the church and of your God, in whose strength have you done it? Is there not One who works all our works in us? Could you work out your own salvation with fear and trembling if God did not first work in you both to will and to do of His good pleasure? How can that, which is itself the gift of God, claim a reward? I think the ground is cut right out from under those who would put confidence in human merit, when we show, first of all, that, in Scripture, salvation is clearly said to be *"not of works, lest any man should boast"*; and, secondly, that even the good works of believers are the fruit of a renewed life, *"for we are his workmanship, created in Christ Jesus unto good works, which God hath before ordained that we should walk in them"* (Ephesians 2:9-10).

"All that I was, my sin, my guilt,
    My death, was all mine own;
All that I am, I owe to thee,
    My gracious God, alone."

Further, if salvation were not a free gift, how else could a sinner get it? I will pass over some of you, who imagine that you are the best people in the world. It is sheer fantasy, mark you, without any truth in it. But I will say nothing about you. There are, however, some of us, who know that we were not the best people in the world—we who sinned against God and knew it, and who were broken in pieces under a sense of our guilt. Personally, I know that there would have been no hope of heaven for me if salvation had not been the free gift of God to the undeserving. After ministering for thirty-seven years, I stand exactly where I stood when first I came to Christ: a poor sinner, nothing at all, but taking Christ as the free gift of God to me, just as I took Him when I was a lad and fled to Him for salvation.

Ask any of the people of God who have been abundant in service and constant in prayer, whether they deserve anything from the hand of God. Those who have most to be thankful for will tell you that they have nothing that they have not received. Ask great soul winners, whom God has honored to participate in the conversion of many, whether they lay any claim to the grace of God, whether they have any merit, or whether they dare bring a price, seeking to buy God's love; they will loathe the very thought. There is no way to heaven for you and me, my friend convinced of sin, unless all the way we are led by grace, and unless salvation is the gift of God.

Once more, look at the **privileges which come to us through salvation**! I cannot, as I value those privileges, conceive that they are purchasable, or that they come to us as the result of our deserving them. They must be a gift. They are so numerous and glorious as to be totally outside the limits of our furthest search and beyond the height of our utmost reach. We cannot encompass any salvation of any sort by our own efforts; but if we could, it certainly would not be a salvation such as this.

Let us look, then, at our privileges. Here comes, first, *"the forgiveness of sins, according to the riches of his grace"* (Ephesians 1:7). He that believes in Christ has no sin. His **sin is blotted out**. It has ceased to be. Christ has finished it, and he is to God as though he had never sinned. Can any sinner deserve that?

> "Here's pardon for transgressions past
>   It matters not how black their cast
> And oh, my soul, with wonder view
>   For sins to come, here's pardon too."

Can any sinner bring a price that will purchase such a blessing? No, such mercy must be a gift.

Next, everyone that believes in Christ is **justified and looked upon by God as being perfectly righteous**. The righteousness of Christ is imputed to him, and he *is "accepted in the beloved"* (Ephesians 1:6). By this he becomes not only innocent, that is, pardoned, but he becomes praiseworthy before God. This is justification. Can any guilty man deserve that? Why, he is covered with sin, defiled from head to foot! Can he deserve to be arrayed in the sumptuous robe of the divine righteousness of Christ, and *"be made the righteousness of God in him"* (2 Corinthians 5:21)? It is inconceivable. Such a blessing must be the gift of infinite bounty, or it can never come to man.

Furthermore, beloved, remember that *"now are we the sons of God"* (1 John 3:2). Can you realize that truth? Others are not, but believers are **the sons of God**. He is their Father, and the Spirit of adoption breathes within their hearts. They are children of His family, and come to Him as children come to a father, with loving confidence. Think of being made a son of God, a son of Him that made the heavens, a son of Him who is God over all, blessed forever. Can any man deserve that? Certainly not. This also must come as a gift.

Sonship leads to **heirship**. *"If children, then heirs; heirs of God, and joint-heirs with Christ"* (Romans 8:17). If you are a believer, all things are yours—this world and worlds to come. Could you ever desire all that? Could such an inheritance have come to you through any merits of your own? No, it must be a gift. Look at it, and the blaze of its splendor will strike all idea of merit blind.

Further than that, we are now **made one with Christ**. Oh, tell everywhere this wonder which God has done for His people! It is not to be understood; it is an abyss too deep for a finite mind to grasp. Every believer is truly united to Christ: *"For we are members of his body, of his flesh, and of his bones"* (Ephesians 5:30). Every believer is married to Christ, and none of them will ever be separated from Him. Seeing, then, that there is such a union between us and Christ, can you suppose that any man can have any claim to such a position apart from the grace of God? By what merit, even of a perfect man, could we deserve to become one with Christ in an endless unity? Such a privilege is out of the realm of purchase. It can only be the gift of God. Oneness with Christ cannot come to us in any other way.

Listen again. In consequence of our union with Christ, God **the Holy Spirit dwells in every believer**. Our bodies are His temple. God dwells in us, and we dwell in God. Can we deserve that? Even a perfect keeping of the law would not have brought to men the abiding of the Holy Ghost in them. It is a blessing that rises higher than the law could ever reach, even if it had been kept.

Let me say, further, that if you possess a **blessed peace**, as I trust you do, you can say:

"My heart is resting, O my God;
    I will give thanks and sing;
My heart is at the secret source
    Of every precious thing."

That divine peace must surely be the gift of God. If there is a great calm within your soul, an entire satisfaction with Christ your Lord, you never deserved that priceless blessing. It is the work of His Holy Spirit and must be His free gift.

When you come to die—unless the Lord comes, as He will—the grace that will enable you to **face the last enemy fearlessly** will not be yours by any right of your own. If you fall asleep, as I have seen many a Christian pass away, with songs of triumph, with the light of heaven shining on your brow, almost in glory while yet you are in your bed, why, you cannot deserve that! Such a deathbed must be the free gift of God's almighty grace. It cannot be earned by merit. Indeed, it is just then that every thought of merit melts away, and the soul hides itself in Christ and triumphs there.

If this does not convince you, look once more. Let a window be opened in heaven. See the long lines of white-robed saints. Hark to their hallelujahs. Behold, their endless, measureless delight. Did they deserve to come there? Did they come to their thrones and to their palms of victory by their own merits? Their answer is, they *"have washed their robes, and made them white in the blood of the Lamb"* (Revelation 7:14). From them all comes the harmonious anthem, *"Non nobis, Domine"*: "Not unto us, 0 Lord, not unto us; but unto thy name give glory, for thy mercy and for thy truth's sake." From first to last, then, we see that salvation is all the gift of God. And what can be freer than a gift, or more glorious than the gift of God? No prize can approach it in excellence, no merit can be mentioned in the same hour. We are indeed debtors to the mercy of God! We have received much, and there is more to follow. It is all of grace from first to last. We know but little at what cost these gifts were purchased for us, but we will know it better by and by, as McCheyne so sweetly sings:

> "When this passing world is done,
>   When has sunk you glaring sun;
> When I stand with Christ in glory,
>   Looking o'er life's finished story,
> Then, Lord, shall I fully know
>   Not till then, how much I owe.
>
> "When I stand before the throne.
>   Dressed in beauty not my own;
> When I see thee as thou art
>   Love thee with unsinning heart;
> Then, Lord, shall I fully know,
>   Not till then, how much I owe."

151

Now, I would like to direct your thoughts in another direction as we consider that **this gift is unspeakable**. Do not think it means that we cannot speak about this gift. Ah, how many times have I, for one, spoken about this gift during the last forty years! I have spoken of little else. I heard of someone who said, "I suppose Spurgeon is preaching that old story again." Yes, that is what I keep doing. If I live another twenty years, it will be "the old, old story" still, for there is nothing like it. It is inexhaustible, like an artesian well that springs up forever and ever. We can speak about it, yet it is unspeakable. What is meant, then, by saying it is unspeakable? Well, as I have said already, Christ Jesus our Lord is the sum and substance of salvation and of God's gift. O God, this gift of Yours is unspeakable, and it includes all other gifts beside!

> "Thou didst not spare thine only Son,
> But gav'st him for a world undone;
> And freely with that Blessed One,
> Thou givest all."

Consider, first, that Christ is unspeakable **in His person**. He is perfect man and glorious God. No tongue of seraph or cherub can ever describe the full nature of Him whose name is *"Wonderful, Counselor, The mighty God, The everlasting Father, The Prince of Peace"* (Isaiah 9:6). This is He whom the Father gave for us and for our sakes. He was the Creator of all things, for *"without him was not any thing made that was made"* (John 1:3), yet He was *"made flesh and dwelt among us"* (John 1:14). He filled all things by His omnipresence, yet He came and tabernacled on the earth. This is that Jesus, who was born of Mary, yet who existed before all worlds. He was that Word, who was *"in the beginning...with God, and the Word was God"* (John 1:1). He is unspeakable. It is not possible to put into human language the divine mystery of His sacred being, truly man and yet truly God. But how great is the wonder of it! Soul, God gave God for you! Do you hear it? To redeem you, O believer, God gave Himself to be your Savior. Surely, that is an unspeakable gift.

Christ is unspeakable, next, **in His condescension**. Can any one measure or describe how far Christ stooped, when, from the throne of splendor, He came to the manger to be swaddled and lie where the oxen fed. Oh, what a stoop of humility was that! The Infinite became an infant. The Eternal was cradled on a woman's knee. He was there in the carpenter's shop, obedient to His parents. There in the temple sitting among the doctors, hearing them and asking them questions. There in poverty, crying, *"The Son of man hath not where to lay his head"* (Matthew 8:20). There, in thirst, asking of a guilty woman a drink of water. It is unspeakable that He, before whom

153

the hosts of heaven veiled their faces, should come here among men, and among the poorest of the poor; that He, who dwelt amid the glory and bliss of the land of light, should deign to be a Man of sorrows and acquainted with grief. It surpasses human thought! Such a Savior is a gift unspeakable.

But if unspeakable so far, what shall I say of Christ **in His death**? Beloved, I cannot speak adequately of Gethsemane and the bloody sweat, nor of the Judas kiss, nor of the traitorous flight of the disciples. It is unspeakable. That binding, scourging, plucking of the beard, and spitting in the face! Man's tongue cannot utter the horror of it. I cannot tell you truly the weight of the false accusations, slanders, and blasphemies that were heaped on Him; nor would I wish to picture the old soldier's cloak flung over His bleeding shoulders, the crown of thorns, the buffeting, and the shame and sorrow He endured, as He was thrust out to execution. Do you wish to follow Him along the streets, where weeping women lifted up their hearts in tender sympathy for the Lord of love about to die? If you do, it must be in silence, for words but feebly tell how much He bore on the way to the cross.

"Well might the sun in darkness hide,
    And shut his glories in
When God, the mighty Maker, died
    For man, the creature's sin."

Oh, it was terrible that He should be nailed to the tree, that He should hang there to be ridiculed by all the mob of Jerusalem! The debased flouted Him, the meanest thought Him meaner than themselves. Even dying thieves upbraided Him. His eyes were choked; they became dim with blood. He must die. He cried, *"It is finished"* (John 19:30). He bowed His head. The glorious Victim yielded up His life to put away His people's sin. This is God's gift, divine and unspeakable, to sons of men!

But that is not all. Christ is unspeakable **in His glory**. When we think of His resurrection, of His ascending to heaven, and of His glory at the right hand of God, words languish on our lips. However, in every one of these positions, He is the gift of God to us. When He comes with all the glory of the Father, He will still be to His people the *Theo Dora*, the gift of God, the great unspeakable benediction to the sons of men. I wish that the people of Christ had this aspect of the Lord's glory more consciously on their hearts, for though He seems to tarry, yet will He come again the second time, as He promised.

> "With that blessed hope before us,
>   Let no harp remain unstrung;
>   Let the mighty Advent chorus
>   Onward roll on every tongue.
>   Maranatha,
>   Come, Lord Jesus, quickly come!"

To me, one of the most wonderful aspects of this gift is Christ **in His chosen**. All the Father gave Him, all for whom He died, these He will glorify with Himself, and they will be with Him where He is. Oh, what a sight will that be when we see the King in His beauty, and all His saints beautiful in His glory, shining like so many stars around Him who is the Sun of them all! Then, indeed, will we see what an unspeakable gift God gave to men, when, through that gift, He makes His saints all glorious, even as He predestined them, *"to be conformed to the image of his Son, that he might be the firstborn among many brethren"* (Romans 8:29).

But we do not need to wait until we see His face to know His glory. Christ is unspeakable as the gift of God **in the heart** here. "Oh," you say, "I trust I have felt the love of God shed abroad in my heart!" I rejoice with you, but could you speak it? Often, when I have tried to preach the love of Christ, I have not been able to preach it well, because I did not feel it as I ought; but more often, I have not been able to tell it because I felt it so much. I would rather preach in that manner always, and feel Christ's love so much that I could speak of it but little. Child of God, if you have known much of Christ, you have often had to weep out your joys instead of speaking them, to lay your finger on your mouth and be silent because you were overpowered by His glory. See how it was with John: *"When I saw him, I fell at his feet as dead"* (Revelation 1:17). If John were to try to explain what happened, he would say, "I could not speak then; the splendor of the Lord made me dumb. I fell at His feet as though I were dead."

This is one reason why the gift of God is unspeakable, because, the more you know about it, the less you can say about it. Christ overpowers us. He makes us tongue-tied with His wondrous revelations. When He reveals Himself fully, we are like men that are blinded with excess of vision. Like Paul, on the Damascus road, we are forced to confess, *"I could not see for the glory of that light"* (Acts 22:11). We cannot speak of it fully. All the apostles and prophets and saints of God have been trying to speak of the love of God as manifested in Christ, but yet they have all failed.

I say, with great reverence, that the Holy Ghost Himself seems to have labored for expression, and, as He had to use human pens and mortal tongues, even He has never spoken to the full measure and value of God's unspeakable gift. It is unspeakable to men by God Himself. God can give it, but He cannot make us fully understand it. We need to be like God Himself to comprehend the greatness of His gift when He gave us His Son.

Though we make constant effort, it is unspeakable, even throughout a long life. Ministers, especially those who have been in one place a long time, sometimes think that they will eventually run out of sermon subjects. If they preach Christ, however, they never will run short. If they have preached ten thousand sermons about Christ, they have not yet left the shore and are not out in the deep sea yet. With splendor of thought, they need to plunge into this great mystery of free grace and dying love. When they have dived the deepest, they will perceive that they are as far from the bottom as when they first broke the surface of the water. It is an endless, unspeakable theme!

> "Oh, could I speak the matchless worth,
>   Oh could I sound the glories forth
> Which in my Savior shine!
>   I'd soar and touch the heavenly strings,
> And vie with Gabriel while he sings
>   In notes almost divine."

But I can neither speak it nor sing it as I ought. Yet I would finish Medley's hymn:

> "Well, the delightful day will come
>   When my dear Lord will bring me home,
> And I shall see his face;
>   Then with my Savior, Brother, Friend,
> Blest eternity I'll spend
>   Triumphant in his grace."

Even in heaven, Christ will still be forever a gift unspeakable. Perhaps we will have a talk together, friends, on this subject when we get there. One good woman said to me, "We will have more time in eternity than we have now." To that I replied, "I do not know whether there is any time in eternity, the words look like a contradiction." "Oh," said she, "I will at least get to talk with you, anyhow. I have never had the chance yet." Well, I dare say we will commune up there about these blessed things when we will know more about them. As we are to be there forever and ever, we will need some great subjects with which to keep up the conversation. What vaster theme could we have than this? In one of his verses, Addison has said:

"But, oh! eternity's too short
    To utter half thy praise."

I have heard simpletons say that the couplet was very faulty. "You cannot make eternity short," they say. That shows the difference between a poet and a critic. A critic is a being with all teeth, without any heart; and a poet is one who has much heart, and who sometimes finds that human language is not sufficient to express his thoughts. We will never be finished with Christ in heaven. Oh, my Lord, Your presence will make my heaven!

"Millions of years my wondering eyes,
    Shall o'er thy beauties rove;
And endless ages I'll adore
    The glories of thy love."

This wondrous gift of God is an utterly inexhaustible, unspeakable subject.

Now, I come to the final point, that **for this gift, thanks should be rendered**. The text says, *"Thanks be unto God for his unspeakable gift."* By this the apostle not only meant that he gave thanks for Christ, but he thus calls upon the church and upon every individual believer to join him in his praise. Here I adopt his language, and praise God on my own behalf, and exhort all of you who know the preciousness of Christ, the gift of God, to join in the thanksgiving. Let us as with one heart say it now, *"Thanks be unto God for his unspeakable gift."*

Some cannot say this, for they never think of the gift of God. You who never think of God, how can you thank God? There must be "think" at the bottom of "thank." Whenever we think, we ought to thank. But some never think, and therefore never thank. Beloved friend, where are you? That Christ should die—is it nothing to you? That God *"gave his only begotten Son, that whosoever believeth in him should not perish, but have everlasting life"* (John 3:16)—is that nothing to you? Let the question drop into your heart. Press it home upon yourself. Will you say that you have no share in this gift? Will you deliberately give up any hope you may have of ever partaking of the grace of God? Are you determined now to say, "I do not care about Christ"? Well, you would hardly like to say that. But why do you practically declare this to be your intention, if you do not want to say it? Oh, that you might now so think of Christ as to trust Him at once, and begin to raise this note of praise!

Some, on the other hand, do not thank God because they are always delaying. In attendance at almost any church service are those who were there ten years ago, and were rather more hopeful then than they are now. "There is plenty of time," you say, but you do not say this about other matters. I admired the children, the other day, when the teacher said, "Dear children, the weather is unsettled. You can go out next Wednesday. But do you not think that it would be better to stop for a month, so that we could go when the weather is better?" There was not a child that voted for stopping for a month. All the hands were up for going next Wednesday. Now, imitate the children in that. Do not make it seem as if you were in no hurry to be happy. As he that believes in Christ has eternal life, to postpone having it is an unworthy and an unwise thing to do. No, you will have it, I hope, at once.

There is a man who is going to be a very rich man when his old aunt dies. He does not wish that she should die, I am sure, but he sometimes wonders why some people are spared to be ninety. He is very poor now and wishes that some of this money could come to him at once. He is not for putting that off. Why should you put off heavenly riches and eternal life? I urge you to believe in Christ now. Then you will be filled with thankfulness and joy.

Some cannot say, *"Thanks be unto God for his unspeakable gift,"* because they do not know whether they have it or not. They sometimes think that they have; more often they fear that they have not. Never tolerate a doubt on this subject, I implore you. Get full assurance. *"Lay hold on eternal life"* (1 Timothy 6:12). Get a grip on it. Know Christ, trust Christ wholly, and you have God's word for it: *"He that heareth my word, and believeth on him that sent me, hath everlasting life and shall not come into condemnation, but is passed from death unto life"* (John 5:24). Then you can say, *"Thanks be unto God for his unspeakable gift."*

Now, dear friends, let me ask you to enter into this exercise. Let us **first thank God for this gift**. Put out of your mind the idea that you ought to thank Christ, but not thank the Father. It was the Father who gave Christ. Christ did not die to make His Father love us, as some say. I have always preached the very opposite. This idea was well expressed by Kent in verse:

> "'Twas not to make Jehovah's love
> Towards the sinner flame,
> That Jesus, from his throne above,
> A suffering man became.

"'Twas not the death which he endured,
    Nor all the pangs he bore,
That God's eternal love procured
    For God was love before.''

God gave his Son because He already loved us. Christ is the exhibition of the Father's love, and the revelation of Christ is made because of *the love of the Spirit*'' (Romans 15:30). Therefore, *thanks be unto God* [the Father, the Son, and the Holy Ghost] *for his unspeakable gift.*''

While you that are saved raise your note of gratitude, be very careful to **thank God only**. Do not be thinking by whose means you were converted and begin to thank the servant instead of the Lord whom he serves. Let the man who was used as the instrument in God's hand be told, for his comfort, of the blessing God sent you through him; but thank God, and thank only God, that you were led to *"lay hold on Christ,"* who is His unspeakable gift.

Moreover, **thank God spontaneously**. Look at the apostle Paul and imitate him. When he sounded this peal of praise, his mind was occupied at the time about the collection for the poor saints; but, collection or no collection, he thanked God for his unspeakable gift. I like to see thanks to God come up at what might seem to be an untimely moment. When a man does not feel just as happy as he might, and yet says, "Thank God," it sounds refreshingly real.

I like to hear such a bubbling up of praise as in the case of old Father Taylor of New York, when he broke down in the middle of a sentence. Looking up at the people, he said, "There now! The nominative has lost its verb; but, hallelujah! I am on the way to glory;" and so he went on again. Sometimes we ought to do just like that. Take an opportunity, when there comes a little interval, just to say, "Whether this is in tune or not, I cannot help it: *'thanks be unto God for his unspeakable gift.'*"

Lastly, as you receive the precious gift, **thank God practically**. Thank God by doing something to prove your thanks. It is a poor gratitude which only effervesces in words, but shirks deeds of kindness. Real thankfulness will not be in word only, but in deed too, and so it will prove that it is in truth. "Well, what could I do that would please God?" you ask. First, I think you could look for His lost children. That is sure to please Him. Go and see whether you can find one of the erring whom you might bring back to the fold. Would you not please a mother if you set to work to find her lost baby? We want to please God. Seek the lost ones and bring them in.

If you want to please God, succor His poor saints. If you know anything of them, help them. Do something for them for Christ's sake. I knew a woman who always used to relieve anybody that came to her door in the dress of a sailor. I do not think that half those who came to her ever had been to sea at all. But, still, if they came to the door as sailors, she would say, "My dear boy was a sailor. I have not seen him for years. He is lost somewhere at sea. But for dear Jack's sake, I always help every sailor that comes to my door." It is a right feeling, is it not? I remember, when I first came to London from my country charge, I thought that if I came across a dog or a cat that came from Waterbeach, I would like to feed it. So, for love of Christ, love Christ's poor people. Whenever you find them, say, "My Lord was poor, and so are you. For His dear sake, I will help you."

If you want to **thank God by bearing with the evil ones**. Do not lose your temper. By that I mean, do not get angry with the unthankful and the evil. Let your anger be lost in praise for the gift unspeakable. Please God by bearing with evil men, as He bears with you. But if you have a bad temper, in another sense, I hope that you may lose it and never find it again.

Lastly, if you want to please God, like the Thessalonians, *"wait for his Son from heaven"* (1 Thessalonians 1:10). The Lord Jesus is coming again in like manner as He departed. (See Acts 1:11.) There is no attitude with which God is more delighted in His saved people than with that of watching for the time when *"unto them that look for him shall he appear the second time, without sin unto salvation"* (Hebrews 9:28).

Beloved, may God enable you to magnify His Son. To Him be all the praise! Let us again lift up our glad hallelujah: *"Thanks be unto God for his unspeakable gift."* Amen.

About the Author

Charles Haddon Spurgeon was born at Kelvedon, Essex, England, on June 19, 1834. His anointing as a boy preacher became widely known, and at the age of 18, he became the pastor of Waterbeach.

In 1853 he was called to the New Park Street Chapel which had been newly erected to hold his services. But the crowds of spiritually hungry seekers were so large that the chapel couldn't contain them. A huge tabernacle was built and opened for services on March 25, 1861. C. H. Spurgeon preached at the Tabernacle every Sunday and Thursday.

Spurgeon became so popular that his Sunday sermons were literally sold by the ton. He appealed constantly to his hearers to move on in the Christian faith, to allow the Lord to minister to them individually, and to be used of God to win the lost to Christ. His sermons were scripturally inspiring and highlighted with flashes of spontaneous and delightful humor.

In his later years, Spurgeon often publicly disagreed with the emergence of modern biblical criticism which led the believer away from a total dependence on the Word of God. He died at Mentone, France, on January 31, 1892.

Through his writings, C. H. Spurgeon has left a rich legacy for the believer who seeks to know the Lord Jesus more fully.